This volume is one of a series of short biographies derived from *The New Grove Dictionary of Music and Musicians, second edition* (London, 2001). The four volumes that inaugurate this series were chosen by John Tyrrell as outstanding examples of the biographical articles in the new edition; they are printed here with little alteration.

Laura Macy
London, 2001

THE NEW GROVE®

# STRAVINSKY

Stephen Walsh

GROVE

MACMILLAN PUBLISHERS LIMITED, LONDON

PALGRAVE, NEW YORK, NY

First published in
The New Grove Dictionary of Music and Musicians®, second edition
edited by Stanley Sadie, 2001

*The New Grove* and *The New Grove Dictionary of Music and Musicians*
are registered trademarks of Macmillan Publishers Limited, London,
and its associated companies

First published in the UK 2002 by Macmillan Publishers Limited, London

This edition is distributed within the UK and Europe
by Macmillan Publishers Limited, London.

First published in North America in 2002 by Palgrave,
175 Fifth Avenue, New York, NY

Palgrave is the new global publishing imprint of St. Martin's Press LLC Scholarly and
Reference Division and Palgrave Publishers Ltd. (formerly Macmillan Press Ltd.)

British Library Cataloguing in Publication Data
The New Grove Stravinsky (The New Grove composer biographies series)
    1. Stravinsky, Igor, 1882–1971  2. Composers – Russia – History and
    criticism  3. Composers – Russia – Biography
    I. Sadie, Stanley, 1930–  II. Tyrrell, John
    780.9'2

    ISBN 0-333-80409-0

Library of Congress Cataloguing-in Publication Data
The New Grove Stravinsky : the New Grove composer biographies / edited
by Stephen Walsh
    p. cm. - (Grove music)
    Includes biographical references and index
    ISBN 0-312-23326-4 (pbk.)
    1. Stravinsky, Igor, 1882–1971.  2. Composers–Biography. I. Title: New
    Grove composer biographies. II. Walsh, Stephen, 1942–  III. Series.
    ML410.S932 N48 2000
    780'.92–dc21
    [B]                                                           00-031122

# Contents

# Abbreviations

## General

A – alto
appx(s). – appendix(es)
arr(s). – arrangement(s), arranged by, for
Aug – August
b - born
b – bass
B – bass [voice]
Bar – baritone
bk – book
bn – bassoon
cant(s). – cantata(s)
CBS – Columbia Broadcasting System
chbr – chamber
cimb – cimbalon
cl – clarinet
coll. – collected by
collab. – in collaboration with
cond(s). – conductor(s), conducted by
CT – Connecticut
d - died
db – doublebass
Dec – December
diss. – dissertation
ed(s). – editor(s), edited by
edn(s) – edition(s)
eng hn – English hn
ENO – English National Opera
ens – ensemble
facs. – facsimile(s)
Feb – February
fl – flute
fs – full score
Ger. – German
gui – guitar

Heb. – Hebrew
hn – horn
hp - harp
inc. – incomplete
incl. – includes, including
insts – instruments
ISCM – International Society for
   Contemporary Music
Jan – January
Jg. – Jahrgang [year of publication/
   volume]
Lat. – Latin
MA – Massachusetts
mez – mezzo
MI – Michigan
movt(s) – movement(s)
MS(S) – manuscript(s)
nar(s) – narrator(s)
NE – New England
NJ – New Jersey
no(s). – number(s)
Nov – November
NY – New York
OH – Ohio
Oct – October
op(p). – opus, opera [plural of opus]
orch – orchestra, orchestral
orig. – original(ly)
perc – percussion
perf – performance, performed by
pf – piano [instrument]
p(p). – page(s)
Ps(s) – Psalm(s)
pt(s) – part(s)

qt(s) – quartet(s)
rec – recorder
repr. – reprinted
rev. – revised
RO – Radio Orchestra
Russ. – Russian
S – Soprano
Sept – September
SO – Symphony Orchestra
spkr(s) – speaker(s)
str – string(s)
sym – symphony, symphonic
T – Tenor
timp – timpani
TN – Tennessee
tpt – trumpet
tr - treble
trad. – traditional
trans. – translation, translated by
trbn – trombone
unpubd – unpublished
U. – University
USA – United States of America
USSR – Union of Soviet Socialist
   Republics
v – voice
va – viola
vc – cello
vn – violin
vv –voices
vs – vocal score
WI – Wisconsin
ww – woodwind

## Bibliographic

19CM – 19th Century Music
BMw - Beiträge zur Musikwissenschaft
BSIM - Bulletin francais de la S.I.M.
   [also Mercure musical and other titles]
CMc – Current Musicology
COJ – Cambridge Opera Journal
JAMS – Journal of the American
   Musicological Society
JM – Journal of Musicology
JMR – Journal of Musicological Research

JMT – Journal of Music Theory
MAk – Muzikal'naya akademiya
MAn – Music Analysis
Mf – Die Musikforschung
ML – Music & Letters
MM – Modern Music
MQ – Musical Quarterly
MR – Music Review
MT – Musical Times
NZM – Neue Zeitschrift für Musik

OQ – Opera Quarterly
PNM – Perspectives of New Music
RaM – Rassegna musicale
RdM – Revue de musicologie
ReM – Revue Musicale
SMH – Studia musicologica Academiae
   scientiarum hungaricae
SMz – Schweizerische Musikzeitung/Revue
   musicale suisse
SovM – Sovetskaya muzika

## Library sigla

Ch-Bps – Basle, Paul Sacher Stiftung, Bibliothek
F-Pn – Paris, Bibliothèque Nationale de France
GB-Lbl – London, British Library

US-Wcg – Washington, General Collections, Library of
   Congress

# List of Illustrations

Igor Stravinsky in the family flat at Kryukov Canal 66, St Petersburg, 1898

Igor Stravinsky in his study at Ustilug, 1913

Igor Stravinsky and Ernest Ansermet

Stravinsky (extreme left) and his wife Katya (extreme right) at the home of Rimsky-Korsakov (seated next to Stravinsky), together with Rimsky-Korsakov's daughter Nadezhda and her fiancé Maximilian Steinberg, St Petersburg, 1908

Autograph MS of the beginning of Stravinsky's Piano Sonata in F♯ minor, composed 1903–4 (*RUS-Mcm*)

Sketch by Alexandre Benois for the final scene of Stravinsky's 'Petrushka', Ballets Russes at the Théâtre du Châtelet, Paris, 1911

Maria Piltz (third from left) as the Chosen One with Russian tribal elders from the first production of Stravinsky's ballet 'The Rite of Spring', Ballets Russes at Théâtre des Champs-Elysées, Paris, 29 May 1913: costume designs by Nikolay Roerich

Stravinsky in conversation with Jean Cocteau

First page of Stravinsky's sketches for 'The Rite of Spring', 1911–13 (*F-Pmeyer*)

Sketch by René Auberjonois for the staging of Stravinsky's 'Histoire du soldat', Lausanne, 1918

Igor Stravinsky: portrait by Pablo Picasso, December 1920

Design by Natal'ya Goncharova, based on the choreography by Bronislava Nizhinska, for Stravinsky's 'The Wedding', Théâtre Gaîté Lyrique, 13 June 1923: pen and black ink heightened with white ink (Victoria and Albert Museum, London)

Page from the autograph MS of Stravinsky's 'Variations (Aldous Huxley in memoriam)', 1963–4 (*US-Wc*)

Closing scene of Stravinsky's 'Apollo' ('Apollon musagète'), Théâtre Sarah Bernhardt, Paris, 12 June 1928, choreography by Georges Balanchine, designs by André Bauchant, with Serge Lifar as Apollo

Igor Stravinsky, Ostend, 18 November 1931

Stravinsky at an orchestra rehearsal, Teatro La Fenice, Venice, 1951

Igor Stravinsky with his son Soulima and Samuel Dushkin Stravinsky in his study, December 1952

Anyone asked to name the greatest musical figures of the 20th century will, almost without hesitation, place Stravinsky at or near the top of the list. Thirty years after his death he remains one of the most extensively performed and influential composers of the century. The colour and exuberance of his first Diaghilev ballets – *The Firebird, Petrushka, The Rite of Spring* – endow them with possibly the greatest appeal to a general audience, but his work touches on almost every important tendency in 20th-century music, from that early neo-nationalism, through the more abrasive, experimental nationalism of the First World War years, the neo-classicism of the period 1920–51 and the studies of old music which underlay the proto-serial works of the 1950s, to the highly personal interpretation of serial method in his final decade. As his work evolved through these distinct styles it produced a flow of fresh masterpieces which continue to repay concentration and attest to his multi-faceted genius.

---

# 1. BACKGROUND AND EARLY YEARS, 1882–1905

Igor Fyodorovich Stravinsky was born at Oranienbaum (now Lomonosov), near St Petersburg, on 17 June (5 June old style) 1882. He was in Russian terms a nobleman; his parents were 'dvoryanine' or, as we might say, gentry. His mother, Anna Kholodovskaya, was one of four daughters of a high-ranking official in the Ministry of Estates in Kiev, a respectable if dull man who educated his daughters in the correct, somewhat prim manner of the provincial 19th century. Anna grew up a good domestic singer and fluent pianist, a well-organized if strait-laced wife and mother. Her husband, Fyodor Stravinsky, whom she married in Kiev (against her widowed mother's wishes) in 1874 when she was still only 19 and he 30, descended from a long line of Polish grandees, senators and landowners. But since the partition of Poland in the 1790s the Stravinskys had come down in the world, lost their lands and gradually migrated southwards into a remote region of what is now south-eastern Belarus'. Fyodor's father, Ignaty, was a working agronomist of vaguely disreputable habits, a womanizer (according to his composer grandson) who eventually left and divorced his Russian wife, and a bad businessman who bequeathed to his youngest son little beyond a determination not to let his own family life disintegrate in the same way.

If there was music in Ignaty Stravinsky's house it was provided by his wife, Aleksandra Skorokhodova, who had an attractive singing voice. But it was probably never a strikingly musical household, and it was only gradually that, while studying law in the mid-sixties in Odessa, Kiev and (when money started running out) Nezhin, Fyodor discovered a talent for singing. Eventually he won a scholarship to the Conservatory in St Petersburg, and in 1876 he made his début at the Mariinsky Theatre (as Méphistophélès in Gounod's *Faust*). By the time his and Anna's third son, Igor, was born (at the nearby Baltic summer resort of Oranienbaum) in 1882, Fyodor had taken the Russian operatic world by storm and was being widely discussed as the finest bass-baritone of his generation.

Music was thus a part of the working environment in the large second-floor flat on the Kryukov Canal, a stone's throw from the Mariinsky, which was to be Igor's home for the next 26 years. Fyodor sang not only repertory parts but also new roles, some written for him, like the Mayor in Rimsky-Korsakov's *May Night*. Leading lights of the St Petersburg operatic world came and went in the Kryukov flat. Fyodor knew not only Rimsky-Korsakov but also Borodin and Musorgsky, as well as prominent music journalists like Nikolay Findeyzen, and conductors like Nápravník. Fyodor also accumulated a large library, partly a bibliophile's collection, partly a working archive of scores and other materials relating to the parts he was studying. Igor inherited his mother's fluency as a piano sight-reader and had access to his father's scores: the Russian repertory, of course (including figures such as Dargomïzhsky and Serov), Mozart, Rossini, Meyerbeer, Gounod, Bizet, Verdi, Boito and the Wagner of *Rienzi* and *Lohengrin*, among many others. A photograph of Igor in his mid-teens shows him at his desk surrounded by the icons of a musical passion, including montages of portraits of the great composers and a low relief of Beethoven. His early enthusiasm for Wagner is attested by a surviving notebook from 1896 with an entry on *Parsifal*: '1877 – wrote text, 1879 – composed opera in rough, 1882 – orchestrated whole of *Parsifal*', with a drawing of 'Bayreuth' in the form of a castle, and information about the dates of composition of *Tristan*. Whether or not Igor attended any Wagner in his youth, he must often in his teens have witnessed his father's performances in a wide range of other operas from the comfort of a family box. He certainly went to the 50th anniversary performance of Glinka's *Ruslan and Lyudmila* in November 1892 (with his father as Farlaf), possibly even to the première production of Tchaikovsky's *Sleeping Beauty* almost three years before that; and ballet matinées must have been a fairly common treat.

Nothing survives, however, of any compositions of his own before 1898, and there was in all probability no talk of a musical career until at least that stage. Early piano lessons with a certain Aleksandra Snetkova were probably no more than a normal part of an upper middle-class domestic education, since Igor (like his brothers) was educated by governesses at home until he was 11. Teenage summer-holiday letters to his parents are more about the books he has read, the plays he has acted in, and the sketches he has drawn, than about music-making. But then music may already have become a touchy subject by the time he was 17; and it is transparent that Igor constructed his letters home, loving as they are, specifically to gratify his parents' expectations.

In the 1890s the family began to spend long summer holidays with Kholodovsky aunts and uncles on their estates in trans-Volgan Samara (Pavlovka) and Ukraine, and after the death of Igor's eldest brother, Roman, in 1897 Fyodor and Anna summered routinely at one Ukrainian estate (Pechisky), where the adored Roman was buried, while Igor and (sometimes) his younger brother, Gury, preferred the other, Ustilug (in Volhynia), where there were lively female cousins and a less funereal atmosphere. This entailed long rail journeys for the boys, for which they were required to account in meticulous detail, and it also meant regular and painstaking health bulletins from Ustilug. Stravinsky's life-long obsession with illness, medicine and doctors doubtless sprang from this source. And it was not wholly unjustified, since tuberculosis was endemic in the Kholodovskys, and Igor and his surviving older brother Yury were both sufferers (to the extent that Igor spent the summers of 1903–4 with his Samaran aunt and uncle at Pavlovka, talking about music – of which they were passionate amateurs – and drinking huge quantities of koumiss, the Tartar fermented mare's milk, which was supposed to be good for the lungs). Like most well-to-do Russians, the Stravinskys also visited German spas and Swiss mountain resorts. Such holidays were traditional and, in some ritualistic sense, precautionary. But in 1902, Fyodor fell terminally ill with cancer, and the German trip that summer was no holiday and certainly no precaution, but a desperate, ultimately unavailing quest for treatment (which included the new Röntgen method). Igor, however, was able to put it to another use.

## 2. TOWARDS 'THE FIREBIRD', 1902–9

Stravinsky had left school (Gurevich's Gymnasium) the year before and entered St Petersburg University as a law student that autumn. His real wish, however, was to study music. Two years before that (in December 1899) he had acquired a new and more high-powered piano teacher, a pupil of Anton Rubinstein called Leokadiya Kashperova. Now, in November 1901, he started private lessons in harmony and counterpoint with Fyodor Akimenko, a newly graduated student of Rimsky-Korsakov; and three months later Akimenko was replaced by the more sympathetic Vasiliy Kalafaty, also a former Rimsky pupil. There is some evidence that these theory lessons were a *quid pro quo* for Igor's agreeing to study law, which in Tsarist Russia was the normal (and reasonably foolproof) route to an eventual sinecure in the civil service. At the law faculty, Stravinsky met and befriended Vladimir Rimsky-Korsakov, the composer's youngest son, and a keen violinist. And it was probably at his suggestion that, in Germany in August 1902, Igor made an excursion from Bad Wildungen to Heidelberg, where the Rimsky-Korsakovs were ensconced for the summer, bearing with him a portfolio of short pieces which may or may not have included the only two works (apart from the fragmentary Tarantella of 1898) which survive from this period: the little piano Scherzo in G minor, and the Pushkin song, *Tucha* ('The Storm Cloud'). Rimsky-Korsakov, who was not given to extravagant praise at the best of times, is unlikely to have been wildly impressed by these gauche miniatures or others like them. But equally he must have been struck by something about them, since he did not (as he is supposed to have done in other cases) simply advise Igor to stick to the law. Instead he insisted that he continue his theory lessons, and agreed to oversee his composition work in due course himself. Significantly, he advised him against entering the Conservatory, sensing that in such an environment the 20-year-old composer would merely be discouraged by his own lack of training.

By the following summer, Stravinsky was at work on his first major task for Rimsky-Korsakov, a sumptuous four-movement Piano Sonata in F♯ minor in the manner of Glazunov (another Rimsky-Korsakov pupil) and Tchaikovsky. In August he travelled from Pavlovka to Krapachukha, in the Valdye Hills to the south-east of St Petersburg, where the Rimsky-Korsakovs were staying that year. Rimsky-Korsakov gave him instruction in sonata writing, and set him orchestration exercises based on his own recently completed opera, *Pan Voyevoda*. Back in St Petersburg, Stravinsky completed the first two movements of the sonata, then broke off to compose a cantata for performance at Rimsky's house on his 60th birthday in March 1904; the cantata was duly performed under the composer's direction, and was described by Rimsky in his diary as 'not bad', but the music has not survived. After completing the sonata at Pavlovka that following summer, Stravinsky soon embarked on his next assignment, a large-scale symphony, which, like the sonata, cultivated good practice in terms of conventional models, the obvious models being again Glazunov and Tchaikovsky. The first draft of the 40-minute Symphony in E♭ came more rapidly than the sonata, and was finished in September 1905.

Stravinsky had been continuing his law studies and living at home on the Kryukov Canal. It was not a comfortable time. Anna had been overwhelmed by her husband's death late in 1902 (according to her great-niece, she kept a photograph of Fyodor in his coffin by her bed for the rest of her life); and she may have resented Rimsky-Korsakov's influence on her son, and its tendency to draw him further into the idea of a musical career. She certainly resented Yury's marriage in January 1904, and cordially detested her new daughter-in-law. On one occasion, Igor fled to Yury's house and stayed there for some days before crawling home to the Kryukov flat. He was also frequently at the Rimsky-Korsakovs', either for his weekly lesson (after which he would usually stay to dinner), or for the regular musical soirées which, early in 1905, crystallized into a formal *jour fixe* every Wednesday, and which his brother Gury, who was developing into a fine baritone, often attended as well. There were also concerts at the so-called Assembly of the Nobility (now the Philharmonic), especially the ever more stereotyped Russian Symphony Concerts, a regular series devoted exclusively to Russian music, founded by the publisher Mitrofan Belyayev, which Rimsky-Korsakov would attend with favoured pupils, often also sitting in on rehearsals. More repertory-based were the concerts of the Russian Musical Society, and (from 1903) the enterprising Ziloti concerts, which introduced new music from the West (Strauss, Elgar, Debussy, Mahler) and were by far the best played. Stravinsky would also sometimes go to the Mariinsky with his teacher, but only ever to opera (Rimsky-Korsakov and his entire circle despised ballet). Rimsky-Korsakov himself was writing mainly operas at the time, and his own premières were red-letter days for all his pupils. Stravinsky went to *Pan Voyevoda* (in the Conservatory) in October 1904, and *The Legend of the Invisible City of Kitezh*, another score on which he himself had worked, at the Mariinsky in February 1907.

It was at Rimsky-Korsakov's Wednesdays that Stravinsky had his own first performances. After the cantata, the Piano Sonata was played by its dedicatee Nikolay Richter in February 1905; and Stravinsky himself from time to time performed short piano pieces and comic songs, none of which has survived. There was also much musical discussion, of works heard at the soirées or at concerts or the opera. But the atmosphere, though in a sense open and stimulating, was aesthetically cramped. New music was discussed, but habitually questioned, and there was a self-congratulatory air to the conversation, dominated by Rimsky-Korsakov's own dry, cynical conservatism, as relentlessly recorded by the diarist of these gatherings, Vasiliy Yastrebtsev. They all also from time to time attended the sole 'alternative' musical venture of these years in St Petersburg, the Evenings of Contemporary Music, an irregular and somewhat ramshackle series of chamber concerts which had started in 1902 and prided itself on breaking the conventional mould of classical concerts in the city. The Evenings were certainly the nearest approach at that time to the modern contemporary music concert, though their programmes were more heterogeneous than strictly ground-breaking, with a scattering of newish French and German works alongside the inevitable rag-bag of Russian pieces old and new. Nevertheless Stravinsky remembered them as the most intellectually stimulating musical events of the time (though he misremembered what pieces of his own they included: only his *Pastorale* and the first of the Gorodetsky songs, *Vesna* ('Spring'), were done before he left St Petersburg in 1910). Here he will have met for the first time the raffish set which included the founders of the concerts, Alfred Nurok, Walter Nouvel (amateur composers, associates of Sergey Diaghilev on the art magazine *Mir iskusstva*, and aesthetes with a reliable passion for the new and strange), and the critic Vyacheslav Karatïgin. Rimsky-Korsakov hated the evenings, partly because they escaped his influence, partly because they stood for everything he disliked: amateurishness, pluralism, contempt (however stumbling) for the rules. As for Stravinsky, nothing more illustrates his own lack of rebelliousness at this time than the fact that, in his mid-20s, he scarcely figured in a local contemporary music series that would have embraced even an incompetent proto-Modernist with open arms.

Russia in 1905 had experienced the first serious tremors of the earthquake which, 12 years later, would destroy the country of Stravinsky's youth. The previous year, the Tsar had embarked on a damaging war with Japan, and 1905 opened with a series of lightning industrial strikes in St Petersburg which culminated in Bloody Sunday (9/22 January), when a peaceful deputation of workers and a crowd of bystanders were fired on in the Palace Square and more than 100 were killed. Like most members of his class, Stravinsky would have been broadly on the workers' side. But there is no sign that he was in any way involved, unlike the firmly liberal Rimsky-Korsakov, who was summarily dismissed from his post after publishing open letters in support of the striking students and advocating the liberalization of the Conservatory establishment. For Stravinsky, the most damaging consequence of these events may have been that the closure of the university in spring 1905 meant he could not take his law finals. His certificates (dated April 1906) show that he never graduated, but merely audited his courses and received a half-course diploma. But whether this was a consequence of the disturbances or of backsliding on his own part is unclear.

A more notable event of 1905, on the face of it, was his engagement in August to his cousin Yekaterina (Katya) Nosenko, the orphaned younger daughter of his Ustilug uncle. Since their first meeting in 1890, he had been growing steadily closer to this softly spoken but intelligent girl, 17 months his senior; and when they married in January 1906 (without the dispensation necessary for first cousins under Orthodox law), it was a love-match which would survive debilitating illness and, on his side, candid duplicities, until her death in 1939. It may have been (as he later claimed) as a wedding present to Katya that, during the late spring and summer at Ustilug, he composed a vocal-orchestral setting of three erotic early poems by Pushkin under the title *Favn'i pastushka* ('The Faun and the Shepherdess').

Meanwhile he had embarked on a radical revision of the symphony under Rimsky-Korsakov's close scrutiny. And it must have been Rimsky-Korsakov who set up the semi-private dry runs of these two works by the Imperial Court Orchestra under Hugo Wahrlich in April 1907 (the Pushkin cycle on the 14th/27th, the two middle movements of the Symphony on the 16th/29th), just as it was Rimsky-Korsakov who in due course arranged for the cycle to be published by Belyayev. Stravinsky later claimed (in *Memories and Commentaries*) that his teacher found the work 'suspiciously "Debussy-ist"'. But this is hard to take seriously, since its main influences are Russian (Tchaikovsky and Musorgsky), and its whole-tone harmonies and tritonal melodic figures standard Russianisms which reflect Rimsky-Korsakov's own contemporary usage. Rimsky-Korsakov does seem to have been disturbed by the Gorodetsky song *Vesna*, which Stravinsky wrote in May or June 1907, and which was sung at a Wednesday at the end of October, along with the little *Pastorale*. But this was mainly because he detested what he regarded as the pseudo-symbolism of the poem, as well as finding the start of the song, the first of many bell imitations in Stravinsky, 'frenetic and harmonically senseless' (see Yastrebtsev's diary entry for 30 December 1907/12 January 1908). The static musette harmony of the *Pastorale* he (or Yastrebtsev) found merely strange. Certainly the main importance of these three vocal works is that they show Stravinsky beginning to make his way, however uncertainly, against the Rimsky-Korsakov tide and, in the *Pastorale* at least, achieving a cool, decorative poise which modestly anticipates the radical thinker of four or five years later.

Meanwhile, having at last completed the revision of the symphony, Stravinsky embarked in July 1907 on a more personal orchestral project, a large-scale scherzo based on a programme derived from Maeterlinck's *La vie des abeilles*. Here he began to explore more freely, and without academic constraint, the 'fantastic' qualities in Rimsky-Korsakov's late magical operas, with their glittering orchestration and spicy harmony based on an eight-note scale of alternating tones and semitones. There were more opportunities to test his ear for such things. In January 1908 his Symphony in E♭ and *The Faun and the Shepherdess* were performed together in a public concert under Wahrlich, and Stravinsky picked up his first ever press notices, which were largely, if not ecstatically, favourable. By the time the Maeterlinck piece, *Fantasticheskoye skertso* or *Scherzo fantastique*, was finished at the end of March, he was a coming man in St Petersburg musical circles. In his *Stolichnaya pochta* review of the symphony, Karatïgin remarked on 'the lively cheerfulness of musical thinking that is characteristic of Stravinsky and distinguishes him to his advantage from many of the newest composers'. Rimsky-Korsakov probably oversaw the *Scherzo fantastique* and he certainly heard excerpts from it, played on the piano by his other star pupil Maximilian Steinberg at a domestic gathering on 12/25 April. But the master was already mortally ill with angina, and less than two months later, on 8/21 June, he died at his country retreat at Lyubensk.

Stravinsky was shattered by his teacher's death. He travelled from Ustilug to St Petersburg (a two-and-a-half-day rail journey) for the funeral. Before leaving, he had completed and dispatched to Lyubensk a new, more compact and refined orchestral scherzo called *Feyerverk* ('Fireworks') – a wedding present for Steinberg and Rimsky-Korsakov's daughter Nadezhda, who had married a few days before her father's death. Now, on his return to Ustilug, he rapidly composed a funeral tribute which he hoped would be performed in one of the memorial concerts that autumn and winter. His letters of the time to the Rimsky-Korsakov family express positive despair at the thought that, amid all the diplomacy and politics surrounding such occasions, his work would be overlooked; the sense of impending rejection is almost tangible. Meanwhile he, Katya and their baby son moved into a new house he had designed on the Nosenko estate at Ustilug, and there he completed a set of four piano studies (begun in May), indebted not to any music of the St Petersburg circle, but to the Moscow composer Skryabin.

At this point, Stravinsky had no fewer than three orchestral works awaiting performance. Ziloti had already seen the *Scherzo fantastique*, had successfully lobbied the house of Jürgenson to publish it, and eventually conducted its première in January 1909. The previous week the *Pogrebal'naya pesn'* ('Funeral song') had at last been presented in a Russian Symphony Concert in Rimsky-Korsakov's memory, conducted by Felix Blumenfeld. Since all the performance materials subsequently vanished, we can judge its character only from reviews. Several critics praised its orchestration, while some regretted that, though often beautiful, it was less tragic in tone than they would have expected: 'the author makes successful play with orchestral colours', one wrote, 'but in itself the piece preserves an impression of artificiality, and is in no way an "outcry of the heart"' (N. Bernstein, *Petersburgskaya gazeta*). If we add to these accounts the common view of the *Scherzo fantastique* as dazzling but insubstantial, we can already sense the local wind blowing against Stravinsky's emerging musical personality. The no less brilliantly ephemeral *Fireworks*, with its subtle fusion of tonal and octatonic harmonies, had to wait another year for its public performance, again under Ziloti, in January 1910. But it was almost certainly tried out at some time in early 1909, perhaps with the Conservatory orchestra, since Stravinsky revised the orchestration extensively in the summer of 1909. But if he himself was dissatisfied with his efforts in this case, others were more impressed.

The first sign was that Diaghilev invited him to contribute a pair of orchestrations to Mikhail Fokine's ballet *Chopiniana*, which he was including in his 1909 Paris season under the new title *Les Sylphides*. Stravinsky had been sketching an opera on Hans Christian Andersen's tale *The Emperor and the Nightingale*, with a libretto by his friend Stepan Mitusov, since at least the previous autumn. But he hastily put this work to one side, and completed the Chopin arrangements well in time for the Paris première at the start of June. Meanwhile Ziloti must have seen, or at least heard about, these pieces, since he too now commissioned a pair of arrangements, of Beethoven's and Musorgsky's settings of the Song of the Flea from *Faust*, for a 'Goethe in Music' concert in St Petersburg in November 1909. That gave Stravinsky time to write the first act of *Solovey* ('The Nightingale') during the summer. He then orchestrated the Musorgsky song and was probably just about to start on the Beethoven when a telegram arrived at Ustilug which was to change his life and with it the whole course of 20th-century music.

The ballet element of Diaghilev's 1909 season, though brilliantly successful as dance and design, had been criticized by the Paris press for its lack of any comparable musical novelty. Diaghilev now proposed to answer this criticism by commissioning, among other works, a ballet on the most typically, exotically Russian fairy tale he or his collaborators could think of, *Zhar'-ptitsa* ('The Firebird'). The process by which this commission eventually reached the largely untried Stravinsky is still obscure (it certainly came by way of Diaghilev's resident composer, Nikolay Tcherepnin, and Anatol Lyadov, and possibly also Stravinsky's old counterpoint teacher Akimenko). Diaghilev's telegram, indeed, was no more than a sounding-out, and the commission was probably only confirmed in early December. By that time Stravinsky had already sketched some music, and may even have had musical discussions with Fokine about the relationship between the music and the action, though the essential scenic details were probably in place by the time he came along.

## 3. THE EARLY DIAGHILEV BALLETS, 1910–14

Igor and Katya, now with two children, had been living for a year in a flat in the Angliysky Prospekt, and it was here, between December 1909 and early May 1910, that the bulk of *The Firebird* was composed. In February the composer broke off for long enough to make arrangements of Grieg's piano piece *Kobold* op.71 no.3 for a charity ball in which a young dance protégé of Diaghilev's called Vaclav Nizhinsky was making his solo début. The piano score of *The Firebird* was then completed on 21 March/3 April, the orchestral score on 5/18 May, and the 45-minute ballet had its first performance in the Russian season at the Opéra in Paris on 25 June.

The spectacular success of this first of a long line of Diaghilev ballet commissions barely disguises now the fact that the music was both derivative and to some extent formulaic. It was true that, at orchestral rehearsals, Stravinsky had to explain the music to the bewildered players, and that, at the first rehearsal, the sonorities were so unexpected that dancers missed their entrances. But this was mainly because of the actual orchestration, in which a huge force was handled with the same wizardry and dexterity that had already been seen in St Petersburg as masks for a lack of musical substance. As music drama, *The Firebird* broke little new ground. The scenario, cobbled together by a committee of Diaghilev's collaborators with Fokine at their head, was an old-fashioned sequence of dances linked by *pas d'action*, much like established ballets such as

*Coppélia* or *Swan Lake*. As for the music, Stravinsky had borrowed the old Rimsky-Korsakov idea of depicting evil or magic in structured chromatics, good or human in diatonics or folksong. His Firebird cavorts to flickering, Skryabinesque harmonies and gasping rhythmic phrases, while the human princesses dance to music that Glazunov himself would not have disowned, and the hero Prince Ivan and his bride are portrayed in Borodinesque settings of 'authentic' folk tunes. The demon Kashchey's dance is infectiously rhythmic; but its phrasing is routine. Of course, Stravinsky's mastery of these varied resources was and remains astonishing (and not only in view of his limited experience). But it might not have portended any outstanding innovative genius.

The success, all the same, was sensational. Overnight Stravinsky became a household name. Socially he was lionized. He was befriended by the Parisian great and good, by Diaghilev's aristocratic backers, by composers like Debussy, Ravel and Satie, by writers like Claudel, Proust, Gide and D'Annunzio, and even by the venerable actress Sarah Bernhardt. It was all very different from the provincial St Petersburg of his experience, with its coteries of Rimsky-Korsakov hangers-on and its so-called 'Contemporaries' evenings. The whole point of the Ballets Russes was that it was a fusion of art forms, and through it Stravinsky was automatically brought into contact with intellectual and aesthetic spheres not restricted by the academicisms and petty politics of a dying musical tradition. He in turn was accepted (including by the Parisian critics) as an equal in this sophisticated and vigorous milieu. In the *Nouvelle Revue Française*, Henri Ghéon called *The Firebird* 'the most exquisite marvel of equilibrium we have ever imagined between sounds, movements and forms'. The fact that this was a general aesthetic, rather than a specifically musical, judgement was, for the moment, of secondary importance.

Whether or not because of his sudden leap to fame, Stravinsky decided to stay for the time being in the West with his family. He spent the remaining summer months in Brittany, composing the two curious Verlaine songs op.9 for his brother Gury (his first ever settings of a foreign language), and tinkering with a new idea for a ballet on a prehistoric subject which he and the painter Nikolay Roerich had already discussed in the spring. But by the time they had all moved in early September to Lausanne (where Katya was to have their third child), he was at work on some completely new pieces for piano and orchestra which soon, perhaps at Diaghilev's behest, became the basis for a whole ballet about the Russian fairground puppet Petrushka. The exact chronology of this change remains controversial. Diaghilev probably manoeuvred Stravinsky into a collaboration with Alexandre Benois (with whom he was making up a recent quarrel), in order to upstage the difficult and arrogant Fokine, who was still, at this point, involved in the new prehistoric ballet – a project, moreover, from which Diaghilev was being excluded. The *Petrushka* subject had certainly been devised, and a good deal of the music written, by the time Benois was directly involved in mid-December 1910. Soon afterwards, Stravinsky paid a flying visit to St Petersburg, and the scenario was worked out in detail. He then returned to Beaulieu, in the south of France, where the family was wintering, and there composed much of the rest of the score. But the extraordinary ending, in which the ghost of the murdered puppet appears above the showman's booth and makes a rude gesture at him, only replaced the original idea of a carnival ending at the last minute. Stravinsky thought up and composed this conclusion in May in Rome, where the company was performing and rehearsing for the Paris season. *Petrushka* finally received its first performance conducted by Pierre Monteux, with choreography by (ironically) Fokine, designs by Benois, and the incomparable Nizhinsky in the title role, at the Théâtre du Châtelet on 13 June 1911.

With the Parisian public, *Petrushka* was as great a success as *The Firebird*, and with musician colleagues like Debussy and Schmitt still greater, though the press, wary as ever of challenges to its *idées reçues*, was more guarded. Once again, it was the integration of elements – music, dance and design – that dazzled balletomanes. But the real source of the work's power was the music. Debussy was fascinated by the 'sonorous magic' of the conjuring-trick scene where the puppets come to life 'by a spell of which ... you seem to be the sole inventor' (letter of 10 April 1912). But there was also a certain boldness, an aggressive self-confidence, which he could also not but envy: 'neither caution, nor pretension', as he wrote to Robert Godet (18 Dec 1911). 'It's childlike and untamed. Yet the execution is extremely delicate'.

This time Stravinsky went straight to Ustilug after the performances, and there began once more to think about the Roerich ballet. But there was still no detailed scenario. This was eventually thrashed out on a visit to Princess Tenisheva's estate at Talashkino (near Smolensk), where Roerich was at work on the interior painting of the chapel. Meanwhile, Stravinsky marked time by setting a series of poems by Konstantin Bal'mont: first a pair of miniatures for voice and piano, *Nezabudochka tsvetochek'* ('The Forget-Me-Not') and *Golub'* ('The Dove'), which can be seen as studies for certain melodic treatments in the ballet, then secondly a choral-orchestral setting of the symbolist poem *Zvezdolikiy* ('Star-Face', but usually known as 'The King of the Stars'). This strange work, distinguished by astonishing chordal sonorities, was finished in short score by the end of September (the full score had to wait until the following summer). Only then, still in Ustilug, did Stravinsky start work on *Vesna svyashchennaya* ('The Rite of Spring'), as the prehistoric ballet would eventually be called. Intensive work continued at Clarens, on Lake Geneva, where the family was once again spending the winter. By the end of February 1912 the first part was complete in orchestral score, and Stravinsky seems still to have been unworried by the need to finish in time for the Paris season. The subsequent postponement

11

until 1913 probably had more to do with Diaghilev's intention to have the ballet choreographed not by the detested (and in any case overworked) Fokine, but by Nizhinsky, who was fully occupied with Debussy's *L'après-midi d'un faune* for the 1912 season, and as yet too inexperienced to be trusted with the hugely complex new work.

At all events, Stravinsky eased up. In the summer, at Ustilug, he completed the full score of *The King of the Stars*; he made an excursion with Diaghilev to Bayreuth, where he saw *Die Meistersinger* and probably *Parsifal* (an experience he certainly found less disagreeable than he later pretended in his autobiography); and late in October he made a brief visit to St Petersburg – his last, as it would transpire, for almost exactly half a century. *The Rite of Spring* was eventually composed to the end at Clarens in November, after which he went to Berlin for the Ballets Russes season, met Schoenberg and attended a performance of *Pierrot Lunaire* (12 Dec). In January 1913 he completed the exquisite *Three Japanese Lyrics*, whose instrumentation for small mixed ensemble perhaps shows the passing influence of Schoenberg's masterpiece. In February he was in London with the company, his first visit to Britain (though *The Firebird* had preceded him the previous June). In March, at Clarens, he added the Part Two introduction to *The Rite of Spring* and worked with Ravel on the score of Musorgsky's *Khovanshchina*, which Diaghilev was putting on in June and for which, in particular, Stravinsky was providing the final chorus Musorgsky had never written. The momentous first performance of *The Rite*, conducted by Monteux and with Maria Piltz as the Chosen One who must sacrifice her life in order to renew the fertility of the soil, at last took place on 29 May in the new Théâtre des Champs-Elysées in Paris.

The riot which attended the première has been much chronicled. It was a typically Parisian affair, targeted as much at Nizhinsky (whose choreography of Debussy's *Jeux* two weeks earlier had been disliked) and even at the theatre's manager, Gabriel Astruc, as at the music, which in fact was largely inaudible. The open, cinema-like design of the new theatre tended to encourage a certain social fractiousness, as perhaps did the hot weather and the presence of a less-than-committed touristic element in the audience. The open dress rehearsal the previous day had passed off without incident before an audience that was actually more typical for the Ballets Russes: a mixture of society – *le tout Paris* – and seriously interested musicians, balletomanes, artists and literati.

Yet the music might well have merited a riot. Certainly it was to remain the most notoriously violent score of a time when huge, noisy orchestras and harsh dissonance were more or less commonplace appurtenances of the new music. The primitive imagery of Russian symbolism, of the kind exploited by Roerich, had always carried a certain revolutionary tone, a note of challenge to ossified social structures. But behind all the racket, behind the wilfully discordant harmonies and convulsive metric irregularities lay a genuinely innovatory kind of musical thinking whose point would not become clear until Stravinsky himself began to deconstruct it in subsequent works. Already *Petrushka* had begun to isolate and manipulate fragments of folk melodies (including tradesmen's cries and factory songs), and to combine them in variable patterns which tended to dissolve regular harmony and metre. *The Rite of Spring* merely intensified these procedures by transferring them to a context where disruption within a fixed, immobile context was actually part of the plot. Both scores make heavy use of ostinato patterns, and both take the idea of a variable-length melodic figure or cell as the determinant of metre. But whereas in *Petrushka* these changing metres are mostly incidents within a prevailing regularity, in *The Rite* they take over the entire rhythmic structure, and even invade the regular ostinato patterns in the form of thrown accents, often drastically emphasized. Because *The Rite* is also more polyphonic than *Petrushka*, there is at the same time a conflicting accentual relationship of the different lines (which is why Stravinsky sometimes found it hard to know where to put the barlines – a problem reflected in the many changes the score underwent in different editions down the years).

Harmonically both works use the idea of modal 'fields'. In *Petrushka* such fields are defined either by the conventional mode of the folksongs, or by the octatonic scale, particularly as articulated by triads an augmented fourth apart, for instance the C major/F♯ major superimposition, which serves as the 'Petrushka' motif, and which Stravinsky explores (and perhaps discovered) as a white-note/black-note separation of the pianist's hands. Octatony is also important in *The Rite of Spring* (along with other, less rational chromatic modes); but here there is a consistent opposition between the melody – often Dorian-mode folksong fragments – and the remainder of the harmonic field, which typically sets up chromatic interferences with it. Stravinsky engineers these interferences by joining together Dorian tunes a diminished or augmented octave (major seventh or minor ninth) apart, as on the very first page. At other times, such intervals serve as constructs in their own right, derived from – or defining – the harmonic field, as in the 'Spring Auguries' or the 'Sacrificial Dance'. They seem a natural expression of the harsh and terrible events the ballet enacts. Yet, curiously, Stravinsky never lost his taste for such chords. What one might call the mistuned octave remained for him an emblematic sonority regardless of dramatic or narrative context, and usually, in fact, without violent or barbaric connotations.

Five days after the première, Stravinsky was admitted to hospital with acute enteritis, which soon emerged as full-blown typhoid fever. He stayed in the Villa Borghese nursing home for more than five weeks, missing all six performances of *Khovanshchina* (only the last two or three of which, however, included his final chorus), the last three of *The Rite* and its ensuing London première (11 July). Instead, he went straight back to Ustilug in mid-July, and there embarked, in

13

collaboration with Stepan Mitusov, on a completion of *The Nightingale*, to a fat commission from the newly formed Moscow Free Theatre. It was to be their last summer at the family home. Yet Stravinsky may already have begun to sense that Russia was finished as far as he was concerned artistically. His first two ballets, given in suite form in both St Petersburg and Moscow, had been greeted by a distinctly mixed press and a deafening silence on the part of his own closest friends (notably the Rimsky-Korsakovs and Steinberg); and now Andrey Rimsky-Korsakov, Vladimir's older brother and recently an even closer friend of Stravinsky's, had published a poisonous review of *The Rite of Spring* in *Russkaya Molva*. The fact that it was apparently partly motivated by fury at Stravinsky's role in the *Khovanshchina* reworking, which had superseded their father's version, will hardly have eased the pain it caused. Paris, by contrast, made handsome amends for its hooliganish first reaction to *The Rite* when Monteux conducted two separate concert performances in the Casino in April 1914, and after the first of these, on 5 April, Stravinsky was mobbed by delirious admirers.

So when the Free Theatre collapsed in May 1914, leaving Diaghilev with the world première of *The Nightingale* (spectacularly designed by Benois) in Paris later that month, the composer was not greatly disturbed, though he lost money by the change. More worrying was his wife's health. In January, after the birth of their fourth child, she had had a severe attack of tuberculosis, which had necessitated a move to Leysin, high in the Alps east of Lake Geneva. And it was here that Stravinsky completed *The Nightingale*, somehow managing to paper over the development his style had undergone since 1909. The change of scene from the forest to the Chinese Imperial court does to some extent justify the drastic contrast between the leafy, moonlit textures of the pre-*Firebird* first act and the brittle artifice of the Draughts Chorus and the Chinese March, and above all the subtly dissonant colourings of the scene with Death. Here at Leysin Stravinsky was visited by Jean Cocteau, who hoped, vainly, to secure his collaboration on a theatre project about the biblical David. The only, oblique, outcome of these discussions may have been the tiny string quartet pieces written that summer. But meanwhile sickness was gripping Europe itself. In July, Stravinsky made a hasty visit to Ustilug and Kiev to consult lawyers about his Ukrainian property, and to collect materials he needed for the ballet he was now planning to write about a Russian peasant wedding. It was the last time he set foot on Ukrainian soil.

## 4. EXILE IN SWITZERLAND, 1914–20

At first, exile seems not to have interfered much with his composing. Though openly and ferociously anti-German, he kept politics well clear of his music. Instead he inhabited a kind of private Russian land of the spirit, working simultaneously on his ballet, a musical setting of authentic wedding ritual texts, and on a number of tiny songs and choruses (*Pribautki*, the *Kolïbel'nïye* or *Berceuses du chat*, the *Podblyudnïye*), related to it in method and material. It was the start of a period of quiet but excited stylistic evolution, comparatively unhindered by travel or major performances. When war broke out in August 1914, the Stravinskys were summering in the village of Salvan, in the Valais. Later they moved back to Clarens, then again back to the mountains at Château d'Oex, from where, in February 1915, the composer made a two-week excursion to Rome to attend the Italian première of *Petrushka*, discuss Diaghilev's new idea of a danced Mass and play him the draft of the first scene of the wedding ballet, *Svadebka* ('The Wedding'). In Rome he also met some of the Futurists, including Filippo Tommaso Marinetti and the sculptor Umberto Boccioni; he saw more of them in Milan in April and heard a demonstration of Luigi Russolo's noise machines. Back in Switzerland, the family at last took a lease on a house at Morges, just outside Lausanne – the first settled tenancy of their married life. They were to stay in Morges (at two different addresses) until 1920. Here Stravinsky became friendly with a group of Swiss-French writers and artists dedicated to a specifically Vaudois, locale-conscious art that would be, in Louis Lavanchy's words, 'audaciously original and candidly unrefined' (*Essais critiques 1925–1935*, Lausanne, 1939): a vision which, to some extent, reflected his own current ethnic preoccupations, though he may have been less interested in their politics, which were pro-French interventionist. Among these writers, the novelist C.F. Ramuz became a frequent guest at the Stravinsky house, the Villa Rogivue, and as Stravinsky's compositions on Russian texts began to emerge, Ramuz took on the task of translating them into French. This led naturally and logically to their collaboration on an original theatre piece, *Histoire du soldat*, a work which clearly reflects the politicized local aspirations of the Vaudois movement.

For the first year or so of the war, Stravinsky worked away at his little songs and choruses, with their tight distillation of the cellular and harmonic field techniques of *The Rite of Spring*, and at *The Wedding*, which was to be an austere ritual in the same mould, but without the spectacular trappings, the fake pre-history, the noise for its own sake and the dense piling-up of counterpoints. The sacrifice here would be vibrant and sociable, not violent or bloodthirsty. The Russian texts, taken from the 19th-century collections of Kireyevsky (and, for the choruses and songs, Sakharov and Afanas'yev) were a crucial part of the new idiom. Stravinsky was experimenting with an idea he later claimed to have extracted from Russian folk verse of a moveable accent, which could be played off against the natural accents of speech, as well as against the musical metre, to make yet an extra rhythmic tier, somewhat like the stresses superimposed on the regular patterns of *The Rite*, but less arbitrary. As for sonority, some concept of the village band seems to lie behind the choices of ensemble. The original version of *The Wedding*, essentially completed in 1917, was scored for a large mixed band of about 40, with only a small string group, much wind, and a battery of percussion and twangy plucked and struck strings, including cimbalom (an instrument Stravinsky became obsessed with after hearing and buying one in Geneva in 1915), harps, piano and harpsichord. There is some echo of this sound-world in the dance piece *Bayka pro lisu, petukha, kota da barana* ('The Fable of the Fox, the Cock, the Tomcat and the Ram'), better known by its French title, *Renard*, which Stravinsky wrote in 1915–16 and sold to the Princesse de Polignac. This, too, is based on Afanas'yev, and seems designed to recreate a type of rustic travelling theatre, with singers and dancers who take a hat round at the end, and a squeaky, clattery band of 15, again including cimbalom. In fact *Renard* remains the key to Stravinsky's wartime quest for an idealized folk modernism, since *The Wedding* was to be drastically altered in sonority, if not substance, by the time it reached the stage in 1923.

Not all the wartime pieces reflect the same quest. Early on (1914–15), Stravinsky also wrote a set of easy piano-duet pieces based on conventional models: a march, a waltz, a polka. A little later he added another set of five (this time with an easy second part) based on various national stereotypes. Stravinsky went to Spain with the Ballets Russes in June 1916, and may have been inspired to write the 'Española' in the *Cinq pièces faciles*, as well as the more disjointed Spanish parody in the study he wrote for pianola – a growing enthusiasm of his – the following year. But the notable feature of these miniatures is their technical resemblance to the Russian songs, even though their material and atmosphere are quite different. They showed how procedures evolved in one stylistic context could readily be adapted to another; in this sense they are prophetic beyond their own musical substance.

Apart from the Polignac commission, none of these works earned Stravinsky any money, and as the war dragged on his circumstances deteriorated. The pianola study was dedicated to a rich Chilean called Eugenia Errazuriz, a patroness of Picasso whom Stravinsky had met in Spain. In 1917 he extracted from his Andersen opera a ballet to be called *Pesnya solov'ya* ('The Song of the Nightingale') for Diaghilev. But Diaghilev was a slow payer, and though the two men struck a detailed contract that summer which included payment for rights in the still unfinished *Wedding*, the problems persisted and led in 1919 to a massive and nearly terminal quarrel between them. It was also in 1917 (January) that the Paris Opéra staged a ballet adaptation of the *Scherzo fantastique*, a production Stravinsky later claimed (mendaciously) not to have been involved in; in fact he would have conducted it had he not fallen ill just before. Soon revolution in Russia would cut him off finally from any hoped-for income from that quarter. In April, a month after the Tsar's abdication, Stravinsky was with

Diaghilev's company in Rome. It was there that he met Picasso for the first time and, for the first night of the season, made his curious transcription of the 'Song of the Volga Boatmen' to be played as a national anthem. *Fireworks* was staged as a light show designed by the Futurist painter Giacomo Balla, but *The Song of the Nightingale*, though ready, was not done. That summer his old German nurse, Bertha Essert, died in Morges, followed swiftly to the grave by his younger brother Gury, who died of typhoid fever at the front in Romania at the end of July. The Bolshevik revolution in October/November merely set the seal on a year of fragmentation and disintegration.

Under these wretched conditions, the idea, hatched early in 1918, that he and Ramuz should write a theatre piece that could tour around and be cheap to perform, with two or three actors, a couple of musicians and a portable stage, may initially have had an economic motive. But if so, it failed dismally. When *Histoire du soldat* was finally staged in Lausanne in September 1918 (with eight musicians, including a conductor, Ernest Ansermet, two dancers and three speakers), it went ahead only thanks to substantial patronage from the Winterthur tea millionaire, Werner Reinhart, and all subsequent performances were cancelled because of the Spanish flu epidemic. Artistically, too, the piece has always had its detractors. The text after Afanas'yev (much wordier in the 1918 version), about the soldier who sells the Devil his violin in return for worldly wealth and a good marriage, has with some justice been seen as moralizing and over-literary. But for Stravinsky the work was important because it enabled him to take stock of apparently unrelated recent tendencies. His score, which could avoid direct concern with the words (since they are never sung), brings together Russian dances of extreme subtlety with modern parodies: a Lutheran chorale, a march, a waltz, a tango and a ragtime (one of several such pieces he worked on at this time). The economy and instrumental brilliance of the writing are throughout astonishing. But the absolute artistic precision which had characterized the recent Russian settings is to some extent dissipated by Ramuz's text, especially as spoken by the narrator, a homely version of an alienation device Stravinsky was to use, and regret, again.

Meanwhile the war had ended, and Stravinsky's circumstances still hardly improved. His in-laws, the Belyankins, a family nearly as large as his own, descended on Morges from Russia and moved in. To try to capitalize on an existing copyright score, he made a new suite of *The Firebird* for reduced orchestra and sold it, illicitly as it turned out, to his new London publisher, J. & W. Chester. He again took up *The Wedding* and started rescoring it for a small but esoteric ensemble of harmonium, two cimbaloms, pianola and percussion. At the same time he wrote a new set of Russian songs with a piano accompaniment that at times recalls the cimbalom (an instrument that does indeed figure in an unpublished version of one of the songs). He also wrote up the *Piano-Rag-Music* for Artur Rubinstein, in return for a cash gift of a year before (already, of course, long since spent). Financially the situation was temporarily saved, in the summer of 1919, by a donation from a group of philanthropic New York ladies, and by a commission from the Flonzaley String Quartet which became the little *Concertino* of 1920. Artistically, it was transformed by a proposal from Diaghilev which smoothly ignored both their contractual quarrel and the unfinished masterpiece that was aggravating it, and sent Stravinsky off in a completely new direction that was to have quite unforeseen consequences for them both.

Diaghilev probably saw his suggestion (in early September 1919) that Stravinsky arrange some Pergolesi pieces he and Leonid Massine had unearthed in the Naples Conservatory as simply a device for bringing Stravinsky back into the Ballets Russes fold until *The Wedding* was ready. He expected another work along the lines of Tommasini's *Good-Humoured Ladies*, based on sonatas by Scarlatti, or Respighi's arrangements of Rossini in *La boutique fantasque*. But Stravinsky, after initial doubts, was taken with the material – not all of it actually by Pergolesi – and was tinkering with it creatively. Meanwhile Diaghilev at last staged *The Song of the Nightingale*, with choreography by Massine and designs by Matisse, at the Opéra in February 1920 (Ansermet had conducted its concert première to a hostile audience in Geneva two months before). This was Stravinsky's first Ballets Russes première, apart from the non-danced *Fireworks*, since the opera itself in 1914. But his true return to the Paris stage was certainly with the 'Pergolesi' ballet, *Pulcinella*, which the company mounted at the Opéra (with Ansermet conducting) on 15 May. Like *Petrushka*, this was one of those rare theatre works which cohere in all their ingredients: Picasso's sparkling neo-*commedia* designs, Massine's choreography and scenario (based on 18th-century examples he had discovered in Naples), and the wonderful dancing with Massine himself in the title role and Karsavina as Pimpinella – everything proclaimed the restoration of the Russian ballet to full form, and in a completely new type of work, with no hint of nostalgia for the old days of leaping Polovtsians or sinuous Sheherazades (even if those old works were still in the company's repertory). Though some questioned the ethics of Stravinsky's recompositions, with their added harmonies, metric displacements and spicy orchestrations, few denied the infectious wit and charm of the result. Reynaldo Hahn, himself a doubter, had to admit (in *Excelsior*) that 'M. Stravinsky has never given proof of greater talent than in *Pulcinella*, nor of a surer taste in audacity'.

One wonders what Hahn would have said if he had known the work which Stravinsky was at that very moment starting to compile from scattered sketches of the past two years, a piece for large wind ensemble which preserved in an almost classical way the most radical principles of his wartime vocal works. The *Symphonies d'instruments à vent*, begun probably in May 1920, is a score which brings to a pitch of intensity the metrical and chord-voicing treatments so typical of those works. Indeed its distillation of a ritualistic Slavonic solemnity is so powerful that Richard Taruskin has plausibly argued that it is actually an instrumental stylization of a *panikhida* or Orthodox funeral service. Study of the sketches and variant scores shows also the extent to which empirical testing – the process that Stravinsky later called 'grubbing about' – lies behind these slow progressions and winding cantilenas. Even allowing for the fact that most of the sketch material of the *Symphonies* was not new, and that the *Pulcinella* material was not original, it remains scarcely credible that these two works can have come from the same pen in the same year.

## 5. FRANCE: THE BEGINNINGS OF NEO-CLASSICISM, 1920–25

In June 1920 the Stravinskys finally moved from Switzerland to France. They spent the summer at the Breton fishing village of Carantec, where the *Symphonies d'instruments à vent* and the *Concertino* were largely composed, then moved in the autumn into the house of the couturière Gabrielle ('Coco') Chanel (a close friend of Diaghilev's patroness, Misia Sert), in the outer Paris suburb of Garches. Here Stravinsky probably worked on a revision of *The Rite of Spring*, which Diaghilev was reviving in December in a new choreography by Massine, then composed the tiny piano pieces of *Les cinq doigts*. In February 1921, the Pleyel piano company gave him a studio in their Paris factory in the rue Rochechouart, and here he worked on the pianola part of *The Wedding*, for a time even envisaging rewriting the entire score for four pianolas. The Pleyel arrangement would later lead to contracts for the transcription of large numbers of his other works for this short-lived instrument, and the studio would survive as his Paris address until 1933, long after the commercial defeat of the mechanical piano by electrical gramophone recording. Meanwhile he and his family moved in May 1921 to Biarritz, where there was an established colony of white Russian émigrés. This was partly, as usual, for Katya's health, but may also have been for Igor's emotional convenience, since Paris at once meant love affairs: first, probably, with Coco Chanel herself, then with the Russian cabaret dancer Zhenya Nikitina, and finally with Vera Sudeykina, the wife of Diaghilev's former stage designer Sergey Sudeykin, who had recently arrived in Paris via Tiflis, and whom Stravinsky had met at the Chauve-Souris cabaret in February 1921. By July, he and Vera were passionately in love; the following spring she abandoned her husband, and from then on the composer led a more or less openly double life apparently with his wife's complicity, though it should be said that the despotic Igor probably gave her little choice and may have led her to feel that without her acquiescence he would leave her and their young family for good.

But it was in Biarritz with his family that he chiefly found the peace and security he always needed for his work. The first major new project, probably dreamt up in discussion with Diaghilev and his new secretary, a 17-year-old Russian poet by the name of Boris Kokhno, was for a short opera called *Mavra*, based on an ironic verse story by Pushkin about a girl in 1830s St Petersburg who tricks her mother into employing a handsome young hussar in drag as the family cook. Stravinsky had been in Spain with Diaghilev at Easter 1921, and in London with him in June, where he heard Eugene Goossens conduct *The Rite of Spring* brilliantly and Serge Koussevitzky conduct the world première of the *Symphonies d'instruments à vent* atrociously (both performances in the Queen's Hall). But *Mavra* was consciously designed as a refutation of this old neo-nationalist Russian style. They had been talking about Tchaikovsky, of whose *Sleeping Beauty* Diaghilev was planning a major revival for London that autumn and for which Stravinsky was to make some necessary orchestrations. And it may be that in discussing the merits of Tchaikovsky (whose music was routinely despised by thinking Parisians of the day, but adored by Diaghilev and his friends) they found themselves considering the whole question of Russian style and of what might be a musical equivalent of Pushkin's mock-banal poem, much of which is taken up with heavy sarcasm at the expense of Romantic self-consciousness about art and technique. Now Stravinsky and Kokhno conceived the idea of a work which would similarly turn the fashionable Russianism of the pre-war Ballets Russes on its head. It would reject the pallid verism and out-worn folksiness of The Five, and replace it with a classical Russianism, referring to Tchaikovsky and Glinka, and cast in an old-fashioned form of set numbers and recitatives, tonal rather than modal (at least by allusion), and with standard oompah accompaniments as in the old ballads still unblushingly purveyed by émigré cabarets like the Chauve-Souris.

*Mavra*, written the following winter (1921–2) and regarded from the first by Stravinsky as one of his best works, has to others often seemed barely to survive the weight of artistic polemic placed on its shoulders. In its style-consciousness, its insistence that (to paraphrase Taruskin) the telling is more interesting than the tale, it must be regarded as the start of that peculiarly Stravinskian neo-classicism in which decisions about style and language are as much a part of the argument as decisions about material and form. In his own mind, this issue was tied up with a certain kind of formalism. Form *was* content; art was a question of order, and to achieve this the artist must stand back, observe his material coolly and objectively, reject the passionate self-promotion of the Romantic com-poser (as well as, he was soon adding, of the Romantic performer). Little of this was understood by the work's first Paris audience in June 1922, who were not helped, admittedly, by the fact that *Renard*, which seemed to be the sort of work Stravinsky was now discarding, had had its première less than three weeks before, and would later run with *Mavra* on the same bill. The opera's polemics, in as much as they were noticed at all, struck Parisians as hopelessly esoteric, and no doubt this was to some extent Stravinsky's intention in choosing the (to Parisians) largely unknown Pushkin and Glinka, along with the 'vulgar' Tchaikovsky, as his models.

He next embarked on an instrumental work which, because its models are more openly those of the high-classical German tradition, and because Stravinsky set out his formalist ideas about it in an article published (in English) in the Brooklyn journal *The Arts* (Jan 1924) soon after its first performance, has been more generally regarded as the start of neo-classicism in his music. With its dry wind sonorities, its highly self-conscious adoption of 'classical' forms and procedures (sonata, variation, fugue), and its sprightly divertimento tone, the *Octet* readily assumed the role of Stravinsky's answer to Cocteau's demand, in *Le coq et l'arlequin*, for 'une musique sur la terre, une musique de tous les jours'. And when the composer himself conducted the first performance in the unlikely surroundings of the Opéra in October 1923, he was anticipating a new career which itself would bear all the hallmarks of an accommodation to the great tradition. Stravinsky had occasionally conducted performances of his own works (the first time ever seems to have been in one of Ansermet's concerts in Montreux in April 1914, when he conducted the scherzo from his Symphony in E♭), but never before a first performance and never yet a whole concert; this happened for the first time a month after the *Octet* première at a concert in the Salle des Agriculteurs, one of a series organised by Jean Wiéner. Nor had he appeared in public as a solo pianist, except in chamber concerts in Switzerland. He was now, however, writing a Piano Concerto of which, in the end, he would not only give the première (in May 1924) but which he would also embargo for five years thereafter. Thus the music in which Stravinsky claimed to expunge the interpreter, a music that pretended to be dry, mechanical and objective, became the basis of his own career as an interpreter.

Meanwhile, *The Wedding* had itself at last reached the stage in Paris in May 1923, in a form which also seemed curiously to co-opt this most ethnically Russian of all his works into a neo-classical sound-world, with its four pianos (actually two double pianos in the first production) and mainly unpitched percussion, together with a constructivist choreography by Nizhinsky's sister Bronislava. This was one of several 'catching-up' premières of Stravinsky stage works during these years in Paris, including also the 1922 *Renard*. In April 1924, the French capital for the first time saw *Histoire du soldat*, having previously heard only the various suites (but this production had been preceded by one in Frankfurt in June 1923, revived at the Weimar Bauhaus exhibition in

August, a performance Stravinsky had attended). The continued appearance of such works as novelties hardly made it any easier for baffled audiences and critics to make sense of the new direction in his music of the 1920s, while for him it was a significant motivation for new work that it kept him several steps ahead of his chic, novelty-hunting Parisian audience.

In September 1924, the Stravinsky family (now including Igor's mother, who had arrived from St Petersburg – now Petrograd – in 1922) moved from Biarritz to an expensive house in Nice. By this time, what was to be his lifestyle for many years had been established. He would divide his time about equally between Nice, on the one hand, and Paris and foreign tours on the other. On the latter Vera would usually accompany him, though sometimes (presumably under domestic pressure) Vera would go back to Paris and the composer would meet up, usually in Switzerland where Katya had relations, with one or more members of his family. In Paris he would mainly work on his pianola transcriptions, though some composition was also certainly done there. Life in Paris would be sociable, gregarious, rich in concert-, theatre- and cinema-going. On tour he would either conduct or play (rarely both in the same concert) nearly always his own music. His voluminous correspondence with concert agents is a whole vast sub-literature in his archive, revealing him to have been an indefatigable and often disagreeable negotiator who could command high fees for concert appearances and who, conscious of his uniqueness, feared no competition. Opinions differed as to his skill as a performer in the 1920s and 30s, but he was certainly good enough to present with reasonable clarity music which, for most conductors, offered a formidable aesthetic challenge (though recordings suggest that the trickier pieces, like *The Rite of Spring* and *Histoire du soldat*, may have been out of his reach technically at this period). On the rostrum he was incredibly vital, athletic, almost balletic, a physical embodiment of his music. In general, musicians respected him and worked well for him, even though there is evidence that his ear in rehearsal was less acute than in composition. As a pianist too he embodied his music. Critics sometimes grumbled about his dry, *meccanico* style. And, like a machine, he could be fallible. He himself claimed that he lacked 'a performer's memory'. But his most famous example of forgetfulness, in the slow movement of the Piano Concerto at its first performance, may be apocryphal, since Prokofiev, who was present, told Myaskovsky (in a letter of 1 June 1924) that Stravinsky had been nervous and had the score on a stool beside him, but 'there were no incidents'.

After the concerto, he worked on two solo piano pieces, the Sonata and the *Serenade in A* (a title not so much ironic as suggestive of Stravinsky's way of looking at tonality, in terms of starting-points and focuses). After completing the Sonata, in October 1924, he set off on two ground-breaking tours: to Warsaw, his first visit for ten years to territory formerly part of Tsarist Russia;

and, early in 1925, to the USA, where he appeared in New York, Boston, Philadelphia, Cleveland, Chicago and Cincinnati, and signed his first recording contract (with Brunswick). In New York he recorded two discs of his 'easy pieces' for piano – not quite his first recordings, however, since an incomplete disc had been cut of the *Octet* in Paris after the première. The *Serenade*, written in 1925, was intended as material for recording under this contract. But no such discs were ever issued, mainly because the acoustic techniques still used by Brunswick were about to be superseded by electrical ones. Stravinsky's own first electrical recordings three years later (of excerpts from *Petrushka*, *The Firebird* and *Pulcinella*) would be with Columbia, in London and Paris.

# 6. RETURN TO THE THEATRE, 1925–34

After playing his Sonata for the first time in public at the ISCM Festival in Venice in September 1925 (two months after the public première by Felix Petyrek at Donaueschingen), Stravinsky embarked on what was to prove his biggest new work since *The Firebird*. In hindsight, we can sense something doctrinaire about the series of instrumental pieces he had composed after *Mavra*, some need to demonstrate how cool, objective and style-conscious he could be. Boris Asaf'yev, the Soviet author of one of the first and best studies of Stravinsky's music, called this 'the synthetic instrumental style of contemporary urbanism'. But *Oedipus rex*, though it shares the style-centred approach of its immediate predecessors, is essentially red-blooded, a theatrical masterpiece by one of the greatest stage composers of his day. There is contemporary evidence for Stravinsky's later assertion that its impulse was partly religious. He had recently been on exceptionally good terms with Cocteau, who had himself been undergoing a somewhat confused religious reconversion through the agency of the Catholic philosopher Jacques Maritain; Stravinsky himself did not meet Maritain until June 1926, but he had read his *Art et scolastique* (1920), with its neo-Thomist plea for order as an aesthetic goal and for artists to return to the medieval ideals of humble, anonymous artisanship. Back in Nice in September 1925, Stravinsky was telling everyone about a miracle in Venice, when an abscess on his right index finger had inexplicably vanished just as he was sitting down to play the Sonata. A few months later, at Easter 1926, he returned formally to the Orthodox communion, to which his parents had always paid lip-service but without any particular commitment or regularity.

Stravinsky told Cocteau (letter of 11 Oct 1925) that he had wanted for some time to write 'an opera in Latin on the subject of a tragedy of the ancient world, with which everyone would be familiar'. The idea was for a monumental, lapidary work of profound seriousness, but in some sense distanced from the

23

audience in much the same way as an austere sacred ritual. Cocteau had some experience of this genre. He had made a modernized French version of Sophocles's *Antigone*; and more recently he had written *Orphée*, a modish, witty predecessor to his famous film of that name. *Orphée* unmistakably lies behind Cocteau's scenic ideas for *Oedipus rex*, as can be seen from a comparison of the prefaces and design sketches in the two publications. But the play's boulevardier witticisms were emphatically not required. For Stravinsky, stylistic ambivalence was not a joke but a way of thinking and feeling. *Oedipus rex* would refer to the past, just as *Mavra* had done, but its models would be of the profoundest and weightiest: Handel, Gluck, Verdi. Sophocles would be glimpsed through the prism of opera since 1600, but he would not be crudely operatized. The characters would mostly be like statues, masked, immobile except for their heads and arms, helpless playthings of the gods, their plight intensified by a kind of music associated with a theatre whose *dramatis personae* are all too mobile, and whose disasters are nothing if not self-motivated.

Stravinsky divided the action into a series of self-contained scenas, linked by narrations for a speaker in evening dress, a kind of self-important museum-guide whose task is to 'remind' the audience of the story as they go along (the device is pure Cocteau, but Stravinsky, who later denounced it, seems to have accepted it without demur at the time). Within these scenas are arias, ensembles and choruses, planned semi-formally, as in the scenes of a Verdi opera. Apart from Oedipus himself and, peripherally, the Messenger, no character appears in more than one scene; but Oedipus's own downfall is superbly charted, from the self-confident embellishments of his vocal lines early on to the stark, unadorned B minor arpeggio of his final phrase 'Lux facta est'. Throughout, the work shows astonishing control of resources and everywhere there is meticulous planning; yet on many levels, things are other than they seem. For instance, the work sees Stravinsky returning to the standard symphony orchestra for the first time (in a new composition) since completing *The Nightingale*; but the strings are very sparingly used, and for whole pages the winds are dominant. The music seems tonally and rhythmically plain by his standards. But the tonality is ambiguous and referential, rather than clearcut, and the metrics are subject to hidden controls; in the scene where the Shepherd and Messenger reveal Oedipus's history, the tempi are entirely governed by a single metronomic unit (a point hardly ever observed in performance). These and other procedures may be seen as equivalents to the Sophoclean concept of dramatic irony. But they are also aspects of Stravinsky's own classicism: modern formalisms that constantly interrogate the conventional forms on which the music appears to be based.

From early on, *Oedipus rex* had been planned as a surprise for Diaghilev in his 20th anniversary season. But the idea foundered on the problem that only

Diaghilev could efficiently plan a performance by his own company. Cocteau fluttered enthusiastically through the drawing-rooms of the Faubourg, but only succeeded in irritating and misreading potential sponsors. Stravinsky kept his head down until the score was complete, by which time it was effectively too late to stage the work, as had certainly always been his intention. So it was given in concert form but as part of the Ballets Russes season in the Théâtre Sarah Bernhardt on 30 May 1927, with the chorus and speaker onstage in front of a black drop-curtain, and the soloists and orchestra in the theatre's long narrow pit ('mon pissoir', as Diaghilev called it). Stravinsky himself conducted, by all accounts not well. Unsurprisingly, the balletomanes had little patience with this earnest and colourless presentation, and Diaghilev himself seems to have disliked the piece from the first. He never attempted to stage it, nor did he tour or revive it, and the opera-oratorio had to wait until the following February for its twin stage premières, in Vienna under Franz Schalk (23rd) and at the Berlin Kroll under Klemperer (25th).

From Paris, Stravinsky went to London, where he played and conducted his first ever broadcast concert on 19 June – it was, he told reporters, his first encounter with a microphone – and conducted a Ballets Russes triple bill. On his return to Nice, he started work on a ballet commissioned by the Library of Congress for performance the following spring in its Music Room, which was being adapted as a small theatre. Stravinsky was told there would be room for 20 musicians and three or four dancers, and he seems at once to have envisaged a serene and statuesque ballet about Apollo, the chief of the Muses, scored only for strings. Work on the score continued at Echarvines, near Talloires on the Lac d'Annecy, where he installed his family for the latter part of the summer (after Katya had suffered an attack of pleurisy in the stifling Nice heat). In October he conducted his 1919 *Firebird* suite at the gala opening of the new Salle Pleyel in Paris. Then he worked more or less uninterruptedly on *Apollon musagète*, as he planned to call it (the eventual simplified title of *Apollo* was Diaghilev's), until it was completed in January 1928.

By this time, Diaghilev was himself in hot pursuit of the new work, which Stravinsky had persuaded him was being designed as a vehicle for his (Diaghilev's) latest flame, Serge Lifar. The Washington production, which duly went ahead on 27 April with choreography by the former Ballets Russes dancer Adolf Bolm (who also danced the title role), was too remote to arouse more than passing concern in Europe. But the Paris production on 12 June was a major event, not least because it was Diaghilev's first new Stravinsky ballet for five years. The choreographer was Georges Balanchine, another recent Diaghilev recruit who had arrived from St Petersburg (by now Leningrad) and succeeded Nizhinska as the company's ballet-master three years before. Stravinsky later described this collaboration as one of the most satisfying in his artistic life; but it was not an exceptionally close one, since Stravinsky was away on tour for much of that spring, and Balanchine was left free to evolve his ideas of an abstract, non-anecdotal choreography, no doubt on the basis of the composer's suggestions, but in large measure free of his interference.

*Apollo* must have startled a Paris audience that still, in spite of everything, thought of Stravinsky as the composer of *The Rite of Spring* (which he had himself conducted for the first time in France at a Salle Pleyel concert only four months before). Here all violence, abrasiveness and even dramatic insistence are stilled, and instead the work coolly and mellifluously depicts the birth and apotheosis of the god of formal perfection in music that is like some 18th-century *ballet de cour* filtered through Adam and Delibes. Yet several critics saw it rightly as a defining moment in Stravinsky's recent work. Boris de Schloezer detected in it a spirit of purity and renunciation, and predicted that the composer's next work would be a Mass, while for Henry Prunières *Apollo* was a flawless masterpiece that revealed Stravinsky's classicism to be 'no longer, as of late, an attitude, [but rather] a response to an intimate need of the mind and heart'. Stravinsky's own mouthpiece of these years, the composer Arthur Lourié, referred to the music's 'struggle against the charm and temptation of aesthetic fetishism', and suggested that Stravinsky's long-cultivated anti-individualism had now brought him 'towards the spiritual, aiming thereby at the long-lost unity of the moral and the aesthetic': Lourié, admittedly, was engaged in a far-reaching polemic setting up Stravinsky as the antithesis to Schoenberg, who had conducted the world première of his Suite, op.29, in Paris in December 1927, alongside *Pierrot lunaire* and other works (Stravinsky himself had not attended these concerts). 'Stravinsky's art', Lourié argued somewhat fancifully, 'is a reaction against Schoenberg's aesthetics'. Implicitly attacking serialism for 'seeking to control the element of emotion and evoke a purified and obedient material', he added that Stravinsky had himself escaped from the apparently comparable prison of neo-classicism, and was now writing music that was 'poly-methodic'.

This description certainly seems borne out by Stravinsky's next ballet, *Le baiser de la fée*, a remarkably inventive montage of pieces by or in the style of Tchaikovsky, set to a scenario (after Hans Christian Andersen) strongly redolent of romantic story ballets like *Giselle* or *Swan Lake*. The work was commissioned by Ida Rubinstein for performance by her new ballet company in Paris in the autumn of 1928, though the idea and the actual choice of some of the Tchaikovsky piano pieces and songs came from Benois, who was also to be responsible for designing the production. But even Benois, one of Stravinsky's oldest collaborators, must have been astonished at the fertility of the treatments, so much more abstracted and varied than those of *Pulcinella* and so alert to the 'freshness, inventiveness, ingenuity and vigour' which Stravinsky had himself proclaimed as Tchaikovskian characteristics in his open letter to Diaghilev at the time of *The Sleeping Beauty* in 1921. Like *Apollo*, *Le baiser de la fée* was substantially composed at Echarvines, where the family summered once again in 1928. But this was for a première in November, and it seems possible that Stravinsky had at first envisaged a more straightforward set of arrangements and only decided on a more compositional treatment at a relatively late stage.

His perennial problem in such cases was his increasing commitment to concert work, which he undertook (whatever *ad hoc* artistic pretexts he may from time to time have mentioned to newspaper interviewers) mainly for financial reasons, to support his large, still dependent and often ailing family and his own high and complicated standard of living. A few days before the première of *Le baiser*, he conducted the new Orchestre Symphonique de Paris in two concerts of his own music, and these were only the first of several Paris appearances that year culminating in the final (as it turned out) Diaghilev season in May 1929, for which he conducted the new Lifar production of *Renard*. There were concerts in Scheveningen, Zürich and Dresden; he went three times to London in May and June 1929, the second visit being the occasion of his last (virtually wordless) encounter with Diaghilev, who died in August having, it seems, not forgiven him for the 'treachery' of working for Rubinstein. Between the two London trips, he played his Piano Concerto under Klemperer in Berlin. This was by no means a heavy programme by his standards. In addition that season he recorded both *The Firebird* and *The Rite of Spring* for Columbia in Paris (having recorded *Petrushka* in London for them in June 1928).

It may have been out of weariness with the concerto, still essentially his only concert item as a player, that he embarked in December 1928 on a new and stylistically very different three-movement concerto which he eventually called *Capriccio*. Here the model (according to Stravinsky himself) is the bravura of Weber's piano sonatas, though in fact the piano idiom of the *Capriccio* often suggests the cimbalom, an instrument prominent in *Renard*, which he conducted that May. For the third year running, the Stravinsky family spent the summer at Echarvines, and most of the new concerto was written there (in reverse movement-order) between July and September 1929. He himself gave the première with the Orchestre Symphonique de Paris under Ansermet in the Salle Pleyel on 6 December. Six days later he signed a contract with the Boston SO, of which Koussevitzky was now musical director, for a symphony in honour of the orchestra's 50th anniversary season (1930–31).

Some four years earlier, he had toyed with the idea of a symphony before abandoning it in favour of *Oedipus rex*. Once again what was presumably thought of initially as an orchestral work now began to take shape in choral terms. That Christmas he jotted down part of the Vulgate text of Psalm xxxix;

and soon he was writing a symphony that was not just choral but severely, even ritualistically, sacred. Aspects of the *Symphonie de psaumes* suggest a sacral neo-classicism: notably the fugal second movement, and the long-breathed tonalities of the finale, in which the regular periods already characteristic of *Oedipus* and *Apollo* acquire a still loftier quality of timelessness and weightlessness. The sense of cadence, so crucial in the finale, is a firmly neo-classical trait. But there is also a powerful strain of Russian atavism in the language. This is his first work since the *Octet* to make significant use of the octatonic scale, and the kind of usage is reminiscent of still earlier works, those of specifically Russian parentage. Stravinsky claimed, in fact, that he originally sketched the first movement to Slavonic words, and there is oblique support for this in the verbal accentuations of the finale (on 'Laudate Dominum'), which shift arbitrarily between syllables as they do in the works to Russian texts. Even the chant shapes of the voice parts sometimes hint at the litany-like repetitions of *The Wedding* or the *Symphonies d'instruments à vent* and the sonorities are similarly dominated by the wind and the piano duo, with the strings represented only by cellos and basses.

As usual, work on the symphony was delayed by concert tours, which included a mid-February visit to Bucharest, where he played the *Capriccio* and met three queens: Marie of Romania and her daughters, the Queens of Greece and Yugoslavia, with whom he and Vera had tea. In Prague on the way home he met the quarter-tone composer Alois Hába, but told reporters that 'I recognize only half-tones as the basis of music' (*Prager Presse*, 23 February). Work on the symphony proceeded in March (starting, as in the case of the *Capriccio*, with the finale), and continued in June in Paris, where Pleyel had set him up in a studio in the new Salle Pleyel building. The symphony was completed in a villa at Charavines-les-Bains on the Lac de Paladru, not far from Grenoble, where the Stravinskys spent the summer of 1930. Koussevitzky had naturally bought the world première as part of the commission; but a delay of a few days to the Boston performance meant that the actual première took place in Brussels on 13 December under Ansermet (the Boston performance was on the 19th). Meanwhile Otto Klemperer, who had been keenly bidding for the European première, may have lost it in the end because of political difficulties which led in early November 1930 to the announcement of the closure of the Kroll. Stravinsky, who was in Berlin at the time, heard Klemperer's world première of Schoenberg's *Begleitungsmusik* (6 November), then a few days later ostentatiously attended Klemperer's *Histoire du soldat* and took a bow with him amid tumultuous applause. He told Berlin reporters that he was astonished at the Kroll's closure. 'In no other city', he told *Tempo* (12 Nov), 'have I and my works met with such interest and understanding as in Berlin, and for that I have above all to thank Otto Klemperer and the Kroll Opera'.

Stravinsky arrived in Brussels in December from an exhausting German concert tour which had had, nevertheless, one creative outcome. In Wiesbaden at the end of October, at the house of his German publisher Willy Strecker (of Schott), he had met the violinist Samuel Dushkin, for whom Strecker wanted him to write a concerto. And the two men hit it off so well that in the next two years Stravinsky composed for Dushkin not only the concerto, but also a large-scale violin-piano duo, the *Duo concertant*, and a series of recital arrangements, including the important *Suite italienne* (based on pieces from *Pulcinella*, the second violin suite Stravinsky had derived from that work). By the end of 1932 they had established a touring duo, with the object of giving concerts in towns which lacked orchestras or the resources (or stomach) to include Stravinsky in their subscription programmes. Meanwhile the showy yet lyrical Violin Concerto, with its suggestion of a baroque concertante style and its crisp tonal harmonies emblematized by the famous triple-stopped chord which starts each of the four movements and which Dushkin initially told the composer could not be played, was completed in September 1931 and first performed by him with Stravinsky conducting the (reputedly very unreliable) Berlin RO in the old Philharmonie on 20 October.

By this time Stravinsky was generally regarded as above reproach by the German press, who in fact took him far more seriously than their Parisian or (especially) Anglo-Saxon colleagues. But voices were beginning to be raised against what Fritz Stege called the 'desecration of Bach ... which, beneath the make-up of French civilisation, reveals clearly enough the savagery of half-Asiatic instincts' (*Zeitschrift für Musik*, December 1931, quoted in Joan Evans, 'Die Rezeption der Musik Igor Strawinskys in Hitlerdeutschland', R 1998). It was an ominous sign of growing xenophobia amid the worsening economic ruins of post-crash, pre-Nazi Germany. When Dushkin and Stravinsky played the *Duo concertant* in a Berlin radio studio a year later (28 Oct 1932), the response was more muted since only the more serious critics would bother to review a broadcast. The subtle change of emphasis, from concertante neo-baroque to a cool and highly abstracted sonata style, escaped notice in Berlin. But Stravinsky's later memory that the duo was inspired by his friend Charles-Albert Cingria's *Pétrarque* was mistaken, since that book only came out in December 1932. On reading it that December, he put aside the Concerto for two solo pianos, which he had been sketching, and drafted a setting of Petrarch's 'Dialogue between Joy and Reason', of which Cingria includes a French translation. This was his first setting of a French text since the Verlaine songs of 1910. But within a month this too was displaced by (and later to some extent incorporated in) a large theatre piece, commissioned once again by Ida Rubinstein, to a text by André Gide about the Greek fertility goddess Persephone. Here the new pastoral spirit in Stravinsky's music would reach its fulfilment.

The first meeting with Gide took place at Wiesbaden, where Stravinsky was again in mid-tour, at the end of January 1933. On the very same day Hitler became Chancellor of Germany, and a few days later a photographer friend of Stravinsky's, Eric Schall, was attacked by Nazi thugs as he walked away from a Munich restaurant with the composer and Vera Sudeykina. It seems possible that Stravinsky himself had been mistaken for a Jew. But this was not his main anxiety where Hitler was concerned (he soon provided Strecker with a detailed statement of his Polish-Russian ancestry). The fact was that in the past few years the greater part of his concert income had come from Germany. But now the booking of foreign artists and the performance of modern music were, at least theoretically, coming under official scrutiny, and in any case economic conditions were such that few organizations could any longer afford even a fraction of his fee. With Dushkin, a Jew, the situation seemed even more serious. And so it proved. Stravinsky's Munich recital with his duo partner in February 1933 was to be his last German concert appearance of any kind for more than three years, and with that single exception (a Baden-Baden performance of the Concerto for two solo pianos with his son Soulima in April 1936), his last public appearance in Germany until 1951.

Stravinsky's essentially pragmatic attitude to the Nazi regime may repel, but it is not direct evidence of sympathy. Though anti-Semitic, like many Russians of his class, he neither advocated nor supported violent or political measures against Jews, and in fact his partnership with Dushkin and high-profile support of Klemperer suggest that the prejudice was to some extent stereotyped and unrelated to individuals. Unlike Wagner, he seems never to have behaved with condescension, or indeed in any noticeably specific way, towards Jewish friends; his frequent and nauseating anti-Semitic remarks come mainly in letters to fellow anti-Semites like Benois, Diaghilev or Reinhart. On the other hand he disliked the Nazis because they brought chaos to his working routine and undermined his income, which aggravated his sense of insecurity as an exile (it was probably for this reason that, in June 1934, he at last took French citizenship). He would certainly nevertheless have gone on performing in Nazi Germany if he had been engaged. He did in fact record his *Jeu de cartes* in Berlin in February 1938, apparently without qualms, and he objected vigorously to his inclusion in the Düsseldorf *Entartete Musik* exhibition the following May on the revealing grounds that it did not reflect the actual standing of his music in Germany (and because it represented him as a Jew).

His attitude to the Fascists in Italy was another matter. Precisely at the time of the Nazi takeover (and possibly even because of the chaos it threatened), he was professing extravagant admiration for Mussolini in newspaper interviews. 'To me', he told the *Tribuna*, 'he is the *one man who counts* in the whole world ....
He is the saviour of Italy and – let us hope – of Europe'. He was received by

Mussolini in Rome that very February, less than three weeks after the Munich incident, and eight months later sent him greetings on his 50th birthday. Yet he knew all about the dark side of Fascism; he knew, for instance, that Cingria had been arrested in Rome on a trumped-up charge in October 1926 and locked up in the Regina Coeli for two months without trial. Later, he knew as much as anyone else about Italian atrocities in Abyssinia in 1936, in which year he sent Mussolini the second volume of his autobiography and expressed anxiety at the absence of any acknowledgement. But by this time the yearning for order and strong government overrode all other considerations.

The desire for order is perhaps the only serious link between Stravinsky's political attitudes and his work. If neo-classicism is an indication of reactionary tendencies, *Perséphone* shares them. But as a specific allegory of ordered seasonal rotation, it can be taken either way. Gide himself was at the time a communist fellow-traveller, and his Homeric play about Persephone's willing descent into Hades to succour 'a people without hope, pale, unquiet and sorrowful' has been seen as a Christianized left-wing tract. But Stravinsky in any case from the start ignored most of Gide's ideas about the work, and effectively ridiculed his graphic concept of the kind of music his words should evoke. For the composer, the text was to be absorbed into the music exactly as in his Russian and Latin works. This, of course, did not please Gide, who, after a run-through at Ida Rubinstein's late in January 1934, fled to Sicily and took no further part in preparations for the production.

This most hybrid of all Stravinsky's works, a mixture of solo and choral singing, *mélodrame*, dance and pantomime, opened at the Opéra on 30 April 1934, with Ida Rubinstein herself in the mimed and spoken title role, and the composer conducting. Though the press treated it with respect, many aspects of the work puzzled its audience. The smooth, almost tensionless third-based harmonies of the first tableau brought to an extreme the composer's apparent retreat from the conventional idea of modernism; and if the later tableaux have more edge, they can also seem more diffuse. Perhaps because of the text, the allusions are French or quasi-French: Gluck, Berlioz, even Liszt, to the point where one might almost detect a conscious accommodation with Gallic culture, with the admiring world of Nadia Boulanger (at whose apartment *Perséphone* had a preview performance a day or two before the première), or that of the poet Paul Valéry, who praised the work's 'divine detachment' in a letter to the composer. The Stravinskys had been living in Paris that winter (after two years in a house in the small town of Voreppe, near Grenoble), and in October 1934 they settled permanently in a spacious, and expensive, apartment in the rue du Faubourg St-Honoré. The composer's Parisianization reached its height just over a year later, when he ran unsuccessfully (and somewhat humiliatingly) for the Académie *fauteuil* left vacant by Paul Dukas's death in 1935. Thereafter, for that and other reasons, it began to decline.

# 7. LAST YEARS IN FRANCE: TOWARDS AMERICA, 1934–9

This brief but intense pan-Gallic phase is marked, curiously, by literary and didactic work. His autobiography, *Chroniques de ma vie*, which came out in two volumes in 1935 and 1936 (ghost-written by Diaghilev's old associate, Walter Nouvel), is a decidedly French piece of literary posturing, rich in tributes and bouquets, silent on important but touchy aspects of his life, and well larded with wordy digressions on aesthetics, in which all his work is seen flatly as the product of a single formalist impulse. The book is often remarkably inaccurate, even about some recent matters. Also in 1935, he introduced the first perform-ance of his Concerto for two solo pianos in the Salle Gaveau (21 Nov) with an extended talk about the new work and the three movements from *Petrushka* (in the arrangement made for Artur Rubinstein in 1921) which Soulima was play-ing on the same programme. Then that winter he participated for the first time in a formal composition class, run by Nadia Boulanger at the Ecole Normale de Musique. Finally, in 1939, came the course of lectures subsequently published in the 1940s as *La poétique musicale*, given at Harvard but in French and essentially a late product of this Gallic phase. They, too, were ghost-written, by Roland-Manuel and Pierre Souvtchinsky.

To a certain extent all this verbalizing was no more than the product of cultural, and occasionally financial, pressure. Except possibly in the *Poétique* there is no overwhelming sense that Stravinsky has anything to say that demands to be said in words, and even there much of the content is derivative, from Valéry, Maritain, Roland-Manuel himself and other critics in the formalist tradition. The most original parts of the 'course' are those which describe the accidental, serendipitous nature of creative work, a concept very much borne out by the composer's own sketches, and by what we know of his working methods, which always hinged on the discovery or 'invention' of sounds at the keyboard. At the end of the *Poétique*, this idea takes the form of the composer as an almost uncon-scious, semi-automatic channel of communication between 'our fellow man ... and the Supreme Being', an idea which Stravinsky later famously re-expressed when he wrote that 'I am the vessel through which *Le Sacre* passed'. But by that time (the late 1950s), such remarks have to be seen as part of a growing tendency, already noticeable in the 30s, to dissociate himself from his Russian background and to foster the image of his early work as somehow sprung spontaneously from nowhere.

Oddly enough, the purely instrumental works of the five years after *Perséphone* are, at first glance, the most conventionally 'process'-based he ever wrote. The two-piano concerto – severe, formal, technically worked out, with its powerful final variations and fugue; the 'Dumbarton Oaks' concerto, a dazzling re-creation of the baroque concerto grosso; and the *Symphony in C*, with its large-scale sonata first movement, its (nearly) standard Beethovenian orchestra and its general affectation of good symphonic manners: these works reflect, in their different ways, Stravinsky's arrival as a 'modern master' whose work had become respectable in mixed company and had lost some of its power to terrify. Both 'Dumbarton Oaks' and the symphony, along with the ballet *Jeu de cartes* (a curiously conventional work, for all its musical brilliance) were American commissions, as were *Apollo* and the *Symphonie de psaumes* before them. They might seem to belong in the well-upholstered concert halls and salons of that last bastion of the private patron, where the composer himself was soon to join them.

His first foray of the 1930s into the USA was early in 1935, when he embarked on his second concert tour of the country, this time a coast-to-coast affair in which he either conducted or accompanied Dushkin in (among other cities) New York, Boston, San Francisco, Los Angeles (where he visited Hollywood studios), Minneapolis, Chicago, St Louis, Fort Worth and Washington DC. The following year he paid his first visit to South America, spending seven weeks from April to June conducting in Buenos Aires, Montevideo and Rio de Janeiro. Meanwhile he had been commissioned by Lincoln Kirstein to write a work for the American Ballet company that Kirstein and Balanchine (now working in New York) had set up in 1935. At the end of 1936 he left France on his third American tour, which began, however, in Toronto in January 1937. Again this was coast-to-coast, and again it combined orchestral concerts and duo recitals with Dushkin, ending in New York with his conducting the première of the Kirstein commission, *Jeu de cartes*, at the Metropolitan on 27 April. It was on this tour that he made the first sketches for what was to become the *Symphony in C*, though whether this was prompted by any hint of a commission is unclear. He also completed the short *Praeludium* for jazz ensemble. But his next work was not the symphony, but a direct commission from Mrs Robert Woods Bliss, of Dumbarton Oaks in Washington DC, for a chamber orchestra piece to celebrate her 30th wedding anniversary in 1938.

The *Concerto in E♭*, known as 'Dumbarton Oaks', was the last work Stravinsky composed wholly in Europe. Much of the first movement was written at Annemasse, at the foot of the French Alps near Geneva, where he and his family spent part of the summer of 1937 in the desperate hope that the mountain air would help Katya's lungs. But as usual, Stravinsky seems to have been able to detach himself completely, while composing, from his emotional and nervous environment, and the E♭ Concerto is one of his most poised and meticulous pieces of writing. The obvious reference to Bach at the start was evidently suggested by the commission, which stipulated a work of 'Brandenburg Concerto dimensions'. But gradually the music departs from Baroque models and though the finale remains superficially 'busy', its imagery becomes fragmentary and kaleidoscopic, in which sense it looks forward to certain much later scores of the American years. It would be interesting to know whether any of this material was originally conceived for the *Symphony in C* which, as eventually written, is in a similar spirit; but evidence is lacking.

Stravinsky returned to the symphony in the autumn of 1938 and completed its first movement the following April. But in the meantime his domestic life had disintegrated. In November 1938 his elder daughter, Lyudmila, who had married the poet and journalist Yuri Mandelstamm in 1935 and had a daughter (Catherine, known as 'Kitty') in 1937, but whose tuberculosis had advanced with frightening rapidity thereafter, died at the age of 29. Then, less than four months later, Katya herself finally succumbed to a quarter-century of exhausting illness. The double bereavement became triple in June, when Stravinsky's 84-year-old mother died. He himself, together with two of his three surviving children, was treated for tuberculosis at the sanatorium of Sancellemoz, in Haute Savoie, where Katya had spent much of her last four years. It was here that he completed both the first and second movements of the symphony, and here that he worked on his Charles Eliot Norton lectures for Harvard the following winter, occasionally visited by the actual author of the lecture texts, Roland-Manuel. In September, three weeks after the outbreak of war, he sailed for the fourth time to the USA, alone.

# 8. USA: THE LATE NEO-CLASSICAL WORKS, 1939–51

The six Harvard lectures were delivered, in French, in the New Lecture Hall (now the Lowell Lecture Hall) in two groups of three: October–November 1939 and March–April 1940 respectively; in addition, Stravinsky also held twice-weekly composition seminars with selected students. In between he conducted concerts on both the East and West Coasts. In January, Vera Sudeykina arrived from Europe, and the couple were married in Bedford, Massachusetts, in March. Later, in the summer of 1940, they went to Mexico specifically in order to re-enter as part of the immigrant quota, filing as they did so for US citizenship (which eventually came through in 1945). Yet another concert tour followed in the winter of 1940–41, including the first performance of the *Symphony in C* (finally completed in April), by the Chicago SO conducted by the composer, in Chicago on 7 November. Soon afterwards they bought a house in West Hollywood, and they moved into it in the spring of 1941.

This was Stravinsky's second emigration. But in many respects it was profoundly, even disturbingly, different from the first. Although by now an experienced American traveller and far from unfamiliar with American ways, he had few friends on the West Coast, spoke only primitive English, and was settling in a region with, at that time, little of the sophistication of 1920s Paris or even pre-20s Switzerland. In their early Californian years, the Stravinskys moved largely in émigré circles. As late as 1948, Robert Craft has noted, 'the language, friends, and habits of the home were almost exclusively Russian ... and so were the doctors, cooks, gardeners, dressmakers'. Their circle included musicians like Szigeti, Rubinstein and Rachmaninoff, Mahler's widow, Alma, and her husband, Franz Werfel, Thomas Mann, the Russian painter Eugene Berman, but hardly any Americans. Money was inevitably short, and although Stravinsky eked out his income with conducting engagements, these were inevitably limited by repertory (his own music being often regarded as dauntingly modern) and by the huge distances between cities. Royalties from Europe largely dried up, and were not adequately replaced by American ones, since the USA was not a signatory to the Berne copyright convention. In effect, Stravinsky was thrown into the market-place in order to survive; and the market-place was not of the kind with which he was familiar.

The problem is reflected in various early brushes with the American publicity machine, but also in his own music of the time. The butchery of his *Rite of Spring* score in the 1940 Disney film *Fantasia* (at which he seems not to have protested at the time) is a famous but not isolated example of the former. Examples of the latter are the *Tango* for piano (1940), which was intended as a vocal work to be supplied with a commercial lyric; the *Circus Polka*, written at the end of 1941 for a ballet of circus elephants, and actually performed in April 1942 in a band arrangement by David Raksin; the short biblical cantata *Babel* (1944), part of a composite work called *Genesis* for which Schoenberg supplied the prelude; the *Scherzo à la russe* written for a broadcast by the Paul Whiteman Band in September 1944; and the *Scènes de ballet*, a 15-minute dance-revue composed for a Broadway show that same year, and doubtless performed there without much regard for textual rectitude (for all the well-known legend that Stravinsky refused to countenance changes). Even several of the works that have come down to us as well-dressed concert scores are supposed to have begun as film music, though documentation on this is so far lacking. Stravinsky claimed, for instance, that the second movement of the *Ode*, composed in 1943 as a memorial to Koussevitzky's wife Natalie, had been planned as music for the Stevenson film of *Jane Eyre*; that the *Symphony in Three Movements*, whose sketches show it to have been composed at various times between 1942 and 1945, includes music written for *The Song of Bernadette*; and that the *Four Norwegian Moods*, a work originally prompted by the Nazi invasion of Norway, was likewise 'aborted film music'.

Admittedly the aborting argues that there were strict limits to the concessions Stravinsky would make to the needs of commerce. Much of the above music suggests a new willingness to write to order; some of the works may accept audience appeal as a criterion of style in a way that would have been inconceivable for the Stravinsky of *The Wedding* or *Mavra*. But all are written to high technical and artistic standards, as if 'pot-boiler' had been taken as simply one more typological category for the neo-classical card index. The way, for instance, in which *Scènes de ballet* avoids, even while it mimics, the vulgarity of the Broadway show is an intriguing illustration of the found object serving as basis for a symbolic discourse that retains its aesthetic autonomy.

Taken as a whole the wartime works are an unusually mixed lot. The popular parodies stand out from the one or two works, such as *Danses concertantes* (a concert piece, not a ballet), or the outer movements of *Ode*, which broadly continue the manner of the 1930s concert pieces in a breezier spirit. But there is also a third strand, represented by the outer movements of the *Symphony in Three Movements*, the two Mass movements (Kyrie and Gloria) written at the end of 1944 some years before the rest of that work, and even the amiable Sonata for two pianos (completed in February 1944), which in one way or another hark back to the composer's Russian past. The symphony thrillingly revives the so-called Scythian, or Dionysian, elements which had been the most famous thing about the early ballets; it was his most 'Stravinskian' work for almost 30 years. No less interestingly, the Mass (eventually completed in 1948) seems to have been a product of a renewed religious consciousness – similar, no doubt, to the one of 18 or 19 years before – itself presumably in some way related to the sense of remote exile. He suddenly wanted to write an austere liturgical work (but for the Catholic rather than the Orthodox rite, since the latter forbids musical instruments in its services). This sent him back to his own earlier ritual music, especially the *Symphonies d'instruments à vent* and *The Wedding*. But it also sent him farther back, to a much earlier church music: to plainsong, fauxbourdon, troping and antiphony. The severity of the Mass is thus by implication linked to a certain archaism of sound and technique, in which respect it looks not only backward but also forward in Stravinsky's own work.

After the end of the war, he wrote two short concertos which, so to speak, sum up his main public styles of the time. The *Ebony Concerto*, written at the end of 1945 for the saxophonist and clarinettist Woody Herman, is to the 'pot-boiling' aspect what the *Concerto in D*, written in 1946 to a commission from Paul Sacher in Basle, is to conventional neo-classicism. Even some of the material is, *mutatis mutandis*, the same. Nor is it at all clear that the conventional piece is superior to the pot-boiler, in its way an immaculate, stylized portrait of the balletic precision of big-band playing, with its five saxophones and five trumpets. But the real stylistic challenge came with Stravinsky's next two works (not counting the already part-composed Mass). Both were major theatre pieces, his first since before the war. And both, on the face of it, implied a kind of *summa* – the master bowing out with classical, large-scale masterpieces in the genre he had dominated since bursting on the scene almost 40 years before.

The ballet, *Orpheus*, was another Kirstein commission, this time for Ballet Society (the forerunner of the New York City Ballet), and it was expressly intended as a pair for *Apollo*, though the two were not initially produced together. In fact the subject was suggested by Balanchine, whose staging of *Apollo* was the touchstone for Kirstein's company. And this time composer and choreographer worked closely together, evolving the details of the scenario and the style of presentation 'with Ovid and a classical dictionary in hand', as Stravinsky recalled in *Themes and Conclusions*. The obvious difference between the two works is that, in *Orpheus*, there is an inescapable minimum of narrative substance, where *Apollo* was hardly more than a series of ritual actions, like *The Rite of Spring*. But Balanchine, who was in general uncomfortable with narrative, leant happily towards a highly statuesque, ritualized handling of the Orpheus legend, and in this way the new ballet seemed to become just the kind of work Stravinsky's admirers (whom in the past he had rarely bothered to placate) expected him to compose.

In fact *Orpheus*, written for a slightly enlarged Haydn symphony orchestra, is a less predictable score than it may seem. Though based, like other Stravinsky ballets, on a stereotyped series of 'classical' dances, it complicates the issue in surprising ways. Most suggestive are the slow framing movements, the introduction, three interludes, and apotheosis, whose severely hieratic tone (intensified by imitative counterpoint, including canon) lends the action a mysterious, repressed quality – the character of a liturgy enacted beyond the iconostasis. Musically, too, it implies a more austere, less conventionalized attitude that was to have its corollary in later works. Counterpoint is here put to work, sometimes with tense harmonic consequences. Stravinsky himself, who was ambivalent about *Orpheus* in later years, praised those parts of the score 'where a developing harmonic movement and an active bass line relieve the long chain of *ostinati*' – implying a criticism of the more old-style neo-classical bass mechanisms, of which *Orpheus* also has a few. More interestingly, he referred to the work as 'mimed [by which he perhaps meant suppressed] song', which made it inevitable, he felt, that his next work would be an opera.

*Orpheus* had its first performance at New York City Center on 28 April 1948, with Stravinsky himself conducting. Just over two weeks before, he had conducted the revised version of his *Symphonies d'instruments à vent* in a Town Hall concert by the Chamber Arts Society, a group run by a young Juilliard graduate called Robert Craft. Unusually, Stravinsky had appeared without fee, as he informed his new publisher Ralph Hawkes, to help Craft and to hear how the revision sounded (he had never conducted the work in public in any form before except for the final chorale, which he had arranged without clarinets to go with the *Symphonie de psaumes* in a broadcast concert in 1945). But the explanation concealed an association that was already unique in Stravinsky's life. He and Craft had been corresponding about his music for some time, and they had met in Washington a fortnight or so earlier. In New York, Craft at once became Stravinsky's shadow, spending every day with him and Vera, quietly absorbing his conversation and personality. Later Stravinsky invited him to Los Angeles, and at the end of 1949 Craft moved into the house in West Hollywood as the composer's assistant, musical interpreter, factotum, travelling companion, Boswell, collaborator, friend, quasi-adoptive son, even at times his musical conscience – a position he was to retain, to the incalculable benefit of Stravinsky's music, but to the fury of many of his friends, old and new, whom Craft displaced or otherwise discomfited, until the composer's death in 1971.

This is not the place for a detailed investigation of Craft's role in Stravinsky's domestic life. Certainly it was enormous, and by no means always placid. For the present purposes it can be subsumed under two headings: cultural and compositional. Compositionally, as we shall see, Craft guided Stravinsky into new waters, technically and aesthetically, and it is no exaggeration to say that without his influence the music after 1951 would have been radically different, perhaps (though of course not certainly) much less vital. Culturally, he transformed Stravinsky's thinking. Hitherto, the focus had been Russian and French; now it became Anglo-Saxon. Craft, by his own description a monoglot New Yorker, instinctively pulled Stravinsky towards English and American literature and philosophy, and towards that American view of things in general which had been so signally absent from the Stravinskys' life since their arrival in the country. Out went the collected Voltaire, in came the complete Henry James. No doubt the transformation was less than total (Craft has said that Stravinsky continued to read Bossuet every day). But it was Craft's practical value as a cultured Anglophone that immediately commended him to the composer, who was at that moment embarking on an English-language opera with a notoriously eccentric but verbally punctilious English poet as librettist.

The idea for *The Rake's Progress* arose from a Hogarth exhibition Stravinsky saw in Chicago in May 1947, and by the time W.H. Auden was co-opted as librettist that autumn, Stravinsky had formed clear ideas of the sort of work he wanted to write. Influences would include Mozart, whose opera scores he requested from Hawkes even before Auden came to Los Angeles for consultations in November 1947. From the start Auden and his co-librettist Chester Kallman understood Stravinsky's need for formal structures, in this case arias and recitatives, strict rhyming and metric schemes, and a high degree of symbolic focus in the narrative. Auden could combine these mechanical functions with the invention of verse of astonishing verbal plasticity and richness. Yet (a crucial virtue in a Stravinsky collaborator) he was apparently untroubled by the composer's sometimes wilful treatment of accent, which was presumably deliberate, since Craft was there to advise him on the correct prosody. On the whole, Auden's rethinking of antique verse forms and patterns is very close to the musical equivalents in Stravinsky's own work, and even the elements of stylization are parallel, which is why the outcome – whatever the work's dramatic or musical shortcomings – is linguistically, in the broadest sense, so harmonious.

*The Rake's Progress* has been criticized as musically too predictable, too much the grand master's summatory neo-classical masterpiece, with its recipe of arias and recitatives (with harpsichord – though a piano was used in the first production) and its rather obvious Mozartisms, suitably coarsened, since this is Hogarth, by a flavour of *The Beggar's Opera*. It has been argued that Stravinsky was too tolerant of a scenario which, while it certainly dealt with the cyclic theme of death and rebirth so dear to his theatrical heart, imported too much generic and sentimental detail, especially into the scenes with the bearded lady, Baba the Turk, and the somewhat drawn-out final scene in Bedlam. But in performance, the opera is nearly always redeemed by the sheer exuberance and variety of its invention, strongest in the parodies of popular 18th-century music: the Lanterloo chorus, the Ballad Tune, Sellem's Aria, and Ann's lullaby. In any case, the summatory aspect conceals some unexpected new directions which show up if we look at the score in the light of what Stravinsky wrote next. For instance, the intensive refrain forms in the final act clearly anticipate the crucial role played by such forms in works from the *Cantata* to *Threni*, where the refrain idea is organically linked to serial method. Not that there is any trace of serialism in *The Rake's Progress* (unless one counts the mocking canon in 'Since it is not by merit'). But if we wish to argue that Stravinsky's adaptation of the method was as much a process of matching as a desperate quest for modernity, it makes sense to see the opera as at least partly a threshold, however firmly shut the door might at first seem.

## 9. THE PROTO-SERIAL WORKS, 1951–9

In all, *The Rake's Progress* took Stravinsky more than three years to compose. It was completed in April 1951, and first performed, after much lobbying and infighting, at La Fenice in Venice (in co-production with La Scala, Milan), on 11 September of that year, directed by Carl Ebert. Stravinsky went to Italy to conduct the première, his first visit to Europe since 1939. After Italy, he conducted in Germany, and heard tapes of new or newish music in Cologne and Baden-Baden, including Webern's Variations, op.30, and works by Schoenberg, who had died in July. Craft has described how disturbed Stravinsky was at discovering that his recent music did not interest the young European composers. Back in California, he wrote nothing for six months; then, in July 1952 (after a second European trip in May to conduct *Oedipus rex* in Paris), he quickly completed the Cantata, stereotyping its form because he was in a hurry to write his Septet. These two works are usually taken as the starting-point for the serial method which informs everything Stravinsky wrote subsequently.

The catalyst for the Septet seems to have been a series of Schoenberg concerts which Craft himself conducted in Los Angeles in the autumn of 1952. Stravinsky attended the rehearsals as well as the concerts, and was fascinated by the music, especially (improbable as it may seem) the Wind Quintet, the Serenade, op.24, and Suite, op.29. The Gigue finale of his own Septet (which like op.29 uses a piano as linchpin between string and wind trios) plainly betrays the influence of Schoenberg's finale. In the Cantata, settings of old English lyrics which connect stylistically with *The Rake's Progress*, there is much pitch-only canon and one item of proto-serialism in the form of a tonal melody ('cantus cancrizans') extended through its own retrograde and inversion forms. No doubt such writing was encouraged by Stravinsky's European trauma. But it is not essentially foreign to his own previous work from the Mass onward, and might, but for what followed, have been accepted as a late-period intensification of that tendency. The Septet is somewhat different, however, because of its systematic abandonment of overt tonality as it pursues its 16-note row through a polyphonic Passacaglia and Gigue (after a first movement based on the same material but candidly in A major–minor and sonata form). Even here the influence of Schoenberg seems to be largely technical. Linguistically, the hard rhythmic articulations and sharply characterized textures seem light years from op.29's contrapuntal self-communings. And curiously, it is through rhythm that Stravinsky seems to restore a new kind of tonal focus, whereas with Schoenberg atonality in pitch and, metaphorically speaking, atonality in rhythm go hand in hand.

The Septet was eventually performed at Dumbarton Oaks in January 1954. By that time several major theatre projects had come, and in all but one case gone. In May 1953 Stravinsky had met Dylan Thomas in New York and they had discussed an operatic collaboration based on Thomas's idea of a rebirth of language and myth after the near-destruction of humanity in a nuclear war. But the poet had died suddenly in November, just as the Stravinskys were awaiting him in Hollywood. Meanwhile in August Stravinsky agreed to write a new ballet for Kirstein to go with *Apollo* and *Orpheus*. Kirstein was floating another Apollonian subject (having previously contemplated Eliot's *Sweeney Agonistes*), whereas Balanchine had had an idea based on Terpsichore which later evolved into a dance competition 'before the gods ... as if time called the tune, and the dances which began quite simply in the sixteenth century took fire in the twentieth and exploded' (letter from Kirstein to Stravinsky, 31 August 1953). It was this last idea that led eventually to *Agon*. But first, Stravinsky composed his *Three Songs from William Shakespeare* and *In memoriam Dylan Thomas*, an intensely beautiful setting of 'Do not go gentle into that good night' for tenor and string quartet, framed by solemn dirge canons (reminiscent of Gabrieli) for strings with trombones. Here a chromatic five-note row is used, without note-repetitions, still using a mainly melodic serialism, whose patterns are emphasized for ceremonial or ritualistic effect – a uniquely Stravinskian touch. The first half of *Agon* was then sketched and drafted, ending in December 1954 with the coda to the 'Gaillarde', which seems to be the first music Stravinsky composed using a chromatic 12-note row. Up to this point the work reflects Balanchine's idea of a succession of antique dances inspired by Mersenne, and alternates tonal pieces with free chromatic dances of a concentrated rhythmic, motivic character. At this point, he broke off to fulfil a commission by the Venice Biennale for a 'Passion according to St Mark'. Only when this work, the *Canticum sacrum*, had been completed (in November 1955), bulked out with a transcription of Bach's Chorale Variations on *Vom Himmel hoch* (March 1956) for the same Venice concert in September 1956, did he return to *Agon* and complete it in April 1957.

*Agon* and the *Canticum sacrum* are often thought of together because both make partial use of 12-note rows, the first Stravinsky works to do so. But only a narrow-minded obsession with the mechanics of serialism could obscure the profound differences between these two works, which are sure evidence, incidentally, that the Stravinsky of *Pulcinella* and the *Symphonies d'instruments à vent* was still alive and kicking hard in his mid-70s. *Agon*, surely, is an astonishing work for a composer who, not three years before starting it, had supposedly been in the grip of a creative aphasia brought on by a terror of stylistic inadequacy. For this score is nothing if not stylistically fearless. It combines Renaissance dances, recognizable yet utterly rethought in movement, tonality and sonority, with a high-speed stream-of-consciousness chromaticism apparently indebted in manner, though hardly method, to the Boulez of *Structures*. It has a galliard in C major built round a strict canon between harp and mandolin with high flutes and double-bass harmonics, propped up by a thick C major chord for solo viola and cellos which breaks every known rule of instrumental voicing. It has an atonal 'Bransle simple' which opens with a rapid canon for two trumpets, and a nearly atonal 'Bransle gay' with a castanet ostinato. It starts and ends in a Stravinskian C major, and its four sections or sequences are linked by tonally fixed interludes which tick over like a car engine while the dancers take up their new positions. But the dances themselves gradually 'take fire in the twentieth century and explode' (notably in the coda to the 'Pas de deux' and the following duos and trios), to the extent that it was long thought that the stylistic discrepancies were due to the break in composition. We can now see that the changes are a reflection of the original subject idea (not clearly retained in Balanchine's highly abstract choreography), and are perfectly deliberate. In fact this is proved by the smooth jointure between the chromatic trios and the final coda, which reprises the opening 'Pas de quatre' with no sense of disruption or incongruity.

The *Canticum sacrum* is no less eclectic in idiom, and hardly less coherent in effect. But in this case the linking concept is not dramatic but ecclesiastical. Stravinsky hoped the work could be performed in St Mark's, Venice (as in fact happened, after a formal approach to Cardinal Roncalli, the future Pope John XXIII, a month before the première). Whether or not Craft's hint that the five main movements are in some sense analogous to the five domes of the basilica is to be taken literally, there is no mistaking the architectural feel to the design in general. The fifth movement is a nearly exact retrograde of the first, the solo tenor's 'Surge, aquilo' is balanced by the 'Brevis motus cantilenae', and the 'exhortations to the three virtues' – Charity, Hope and Faith – themselves form a central arch or dome for the whole structure. Many incidental details show that Stravinsky was thinking historically about Venice, and acoustically about a large reverberant church (though whether he allowed adequately for the profound and interminable echo of St Mark's itself is a question only those who attended the first performance can answer). The 'Euntes in mundum' and its retrograde have an unmistakably Venetian ring, with their organ versets, and their *stile concitato* note-repetitions for quartets of trumpets and trombones. The versets, soft and slow, allow the ensemble echoes to clear between sections. By contrast the central movements, with their chromatic, sometimes canonic, lines, have a more intimate quality, and the versets suggest a dialogue, or verse and response form. The *Canticum* shares one other new quality with *Agon*, its extreme, even abrupt concision, which (except in the *stile concitato* episodes) largely does away with the varied ostinato repetitions so characteristic of Stravinsky's earlier manners.

In Berlin in early October 1956, three weeks after the *Canticum sacrum* première, Stravinsky suffered a stroke while conducting the *Symphony in C*. Curiously enough, though alarming at the time, it seems not to have demanded any serious reduction in his work-rate, which actually increased thereafter, at least in the sense that his schedule of conducting tours continued to grow for another five or six years (though he conducted less in each concert, while Craft conducted more). Soon after the stroke, he was diagnosed with polycythemia. For the remaining 15 years of his life, health and health-care were to be his main preoccupation outside music, as well as the greatest strain on his exchequer, which explains why he continued to tour and conduct all over the world for long after it can have been medically (to say nothing of artistically) sensible to do so. He simply could not afford to stop. Not until after his concert in Toronto in May 1967, at which he conducted (sitting down, Craft says, for the first time ever) the suite from *Pulcinella*, did he at last decide that the time had come to call a halt.

After the concert première of *Agon*, conducted by Craft in Los Angeles in June 1957 (the stage première followed in New York in early December), Stravinsky returned to Venice; and there in August, in the cellar club of the Hotel Bauer Grünwald, he started work on another sacred work with covert Venetian connections, a setting of texts from the *Lamentations of Jeremiah*. *Threni*, which he completed the following March and conducted in the upper chamber of the Scuola Grande di San Rocco on 23 September 1958, is famous in the Stravinsky literature as his first score entirely based on a 12-note row. It remains, nevertheless, one of his least known works, seldom performed and little recorded, no doubt mainly because of intonational difficulties for the chorus and (especially) the vocal soloists, who sing for much of the time unaccompanied. Though not consistently atonal in the Schoenbergian sense, since Stravinsky seeks out quasi-tonal areas of agreement and consonance between row-forms and different contrapuntal voices, it is intervallically severe, and the harmonic intersections remain, in tonal terms, grammatically arbitrary.

Technically, *Threni* continues to redefine serialism in Stravinsky's own image. The row is still treated linearly, as if it were a folksong or a plainchant. Sometimes it is divided into cells, as in *The Rite of Spring* or *The Wedding*. Sometimes, by contrast, it is used in effect like a complete theme. Many passages are coterminous with (often canonic) statements of the row, and here and there Stravinsky rotates the row, moving its first few notes to the end, without any far-reaching implications. There is, undoubtedly, a certain pedantry in such procedures. But they also suggest some idea of 'litany' as a highly ordered and repetitive phenomenon whose patterning is transparent by its nature. The result is a work of extreme and possibly self-defeating severity: a long work by the standards of late Stravinsky (about 35 minutes), and in colouring exceptionally dark, with clarinets and horns prominent in their lower registers, sarrusophone, trombones and tuba but no trumpets (except for the strangely heraldic flugelhorn solo in the 'Quomodo sedet'), and piano and harp written exclusively in the bass clef until the final section. Not surprisingly, performances have been rare and usually unsatisfactory. It was at the Paris première, conducted by the composer in a Domaine Musical concert on 14 November 1958, that the work was so badly sung and played that the audience jeered, a failure Stravinsky attributed to poor preparation on the part of Pierre Boulez.

Boulez and Stravinsky had for a time been close in the mid-1950s, and Boulez's influence – or at least that of the tendency of which he was by that time the acknowledged leader – is noticeable in the series of published conversations with Craft which began at the time of *Threni*. This is particularly true of the first volume (*Conversations with Igor Stravinsky*), with its discussions of technical and aesthetic questions, and its famous metro-map drawing of Stravinsky's latest style. The memoir-orientated later volumes retreat somewhat from the regrettably subservient positions of the first, but are still inclined to be apologetic about those earlier (especially neo-classical) works of his most despised by the ferocious avant-gardists of the day. Craft has admitted that the form and in many cases the language of these volumes, which include excerpts from his own diaries and, in the last book, 'interviews' obviously written by him, are his work, but has always maintained that the substance, noted down from replies or remarks made by Stravinsky under all kinds of circumstances, is authentic. Some tendencies in the books obviously reflect Craft's influence, but then so did Stravinsky's own thinking at this time. Two facts are clear: first, that the books are historically very unreliable and inaccurate, especially (though not only) about Stravinsky's Russian life and friendships; secondly, that they are brilliantly vivid, entertaining, and compulsively readable – perhaps the best books of their kind by or about a musician since Berlioz's *Memoirs*.

## 10. FINAL YEARS, 1959–71

If the hypermodernist influence on Stravinsky's opinions retreated somewhat after *Conversations*, the effect on his music if anything increased. *Movements* for piano and orchestra, commissioned by a Swiss industrialist called Karl Weber for his pianist wife in March 1958, may be less severe than *Threni* in the hieratic sense, but it is a great deal more hermetic in point of style and technique. Here Stravinsky converts the seemingly inconsequential row rotations of the earlier work into a complex note-generating programme, which involves 'reading off' chords and melodies from a grid made out of rotated row forms stacked on top of one another (a technique partly derived, it seems, from his friend Ernst Krenek's own setting of *Lamentations*). To some extent this method may appear no more than a useful way of spinning notes which can then be processed rhythmically, texturally and in other ways. But that may be to underrate the possible symbolism of such schemes for a mind like Stravinsky's. Nearly all his subsequent works are religious, and nearly all use rotation grids in some more or less esoteric combination with sacred texts.

The obvious major exception is the *Monumentum pro Gesualdo di Venosa*, a free recomposition of a trio of Gesualdo madrigals for a small mixed ensemble of instruments, made in March 1960 two months after the première in New York of *Movements*. Stravinsky had already made completions of three Gesualdo motets, versions which, despite their somewhat speculative nature, were included by Glenn Watkins in his and Weismann's Gesualdo edition (Hamburg, 1957–67). Vocal music of the Renaissance and pre-Renaissance was another enthusiasm of

Craft's whose influence can be detected in Stravinsky's later works. The 'Venetian' works of the 1950s were written in the shadow of various performances by Craft of Monteverdi (including the Vespers), Schütz, the Gabrielis and others; and *Threni*, additionally, after hearing Craft conduct Tallis's *Lamentations* at the Monday Evening Concerts in Los Angeles. Isaac, Josquin, Machaut and Ockeghem also figured in these concerts. It seems obvious that both the sound of such music and its often intricate canonic and isorhythmic structures were in Stravinsky's mind as he turned to the composition of his last few sacred vocal and choral works.

An example is the 'Prayer' movement of *A Sermon, a Narrative and a Prayer*, completed in January 1961, and first performed in Basle just over a year later under Paul Sacher, who had commissioned it. The setting of Thomas Dekker's 'Oh My God, if it Bee Thy Pleasure' for choir and solo voices accompanied by a tocsin-like combination of gongs, piano, harp and double-bass has an intensity of feeling which arises audibly from the concentrated polyphony of the writing, but surely also (not so audibly) from the fact that all the actual notes come from a hexachordal rotation grid. The grid operates throughout the work, indeed, providing schematic support (not, one hopes, in any ironical spirit) for St Paul's 'We are saved by hope' in the 'Sermon', and for the account – part-spoken, part-sung – of St Stephen's martyrdom at Paul's hands in the central 'Narrative'.

Stravinsky had by this time already conceived the idea for *The Flood*, and may consciously have used the St Stephen narrative as a study for the more complex narrations he envisaged for the later work, which he was writing for television. By far the most brilliant and varied Stravinsky score after *Agon*, *The Flood* suffered from the diffuseness demanded by the popular medium; it had to be anecdotal, picturesque, graphic – qualities which Stravinsky had long since abandoned in stage ballets. 'The subject of *The Flood*', he remarked during discussions with Balanchine, who was choreographing the production, 'is not the Noah story ... but Sin'; and Robert Craft's adaptation of the Chester and York Mystery Plays duly embraces the whole Old and New Testament cosmology from the Fall to the Redemption in a brisk, emblematic 25 minutes, which, for the transmission on 14 June 1962, CBS extended to an hour with the help of an introductory talk about Flood myths, and various interruptions for commercials by the sponsor, Breck Shampoo – surely the apotheosis of targeted marketing. Perhaps luckily, Stravinsky did not see the telecast, as he was in Rome on his way to Hamburg for his 80th birthday celebrations.

However eventful the TV production may have been, the music made few concessions to its popular audience. Although the trappings of post-Webernian serialism are applied with unerring wit, it is a wit that requires musical sophistication for its understanding. To see the joke of an ark being built with sharp serial nails then carried away on a flood of rotating waves (preceded by a flicker

45

of combinatorial lightning), one perhaps needs at least to have heard, if not enjoyed, other, more sombre work in this genre. For any such listener, though, *The Flood* was invigorating proof than in his 80th year Stravinsky had lost none of his creative energy. Though in a sense bitty and short-winded, the music has a centripetal speed which holds it together, from the serial Jacob's ladder of the Prelude through to the so-called 'Prolepsis [foretelling] of Christianity', ending with the same ladder translated into an image of the Redemption. In between, the work falters only during the spoken narrations, which here (as in *Babel* and unlike in *Oedipus rex*) are simply a device for getting through the story, with no oblique or ironic intention. How would Stravinsky and Balanchine have handled such a scenario in a ballet composed for the theatre? One feels that the result would have been more concentrated, more abstract and, probably, simpler.

In fact his next work, *Abraham and Isaac*, gives a clear indication of his late feeling for biblical treatment when external factors did not obtrude. The inspiration for this strangely hermetic masterpiece, for baritone solo and chamber ensemble, seems to have been hearing Isaiah Berlin read biblical Hebrew one day in Oxford in 1961, and by the time Stravinsky made his first visit to Israel at the end of August 1962, the composition was already in hand. Only at this stage was it commissioned. After the Israel trip came the momentous visit to the Soviet Union, in September and October 1962, the first time he had set foot on Russian soil proper since October 1912. It was momentous, of course, psychologically rather than artistically. According to Craft, who accompanied them, the Stravinskys were profoundly moved by the visit, reverting swiftly to an instinctive Russianism and turning a blind eye to the inconveniences and discomforts of Soviet life. 'Their abiding emotion', he recorded in his *Chronicle of a Friendship* (1994), was 'their deep love of, and pride in, everything Russian'. The composer conducted concerts in Moscow and Leningrad that included *Fireworks*, *Petrushka*, *The Rite of Spring*, *Ode* and *Orpheus*. Craft noted that the chief attraction for the audiences was the composer himself, rather than the music, much of it still unfamiliar and difficult for them. But the playing of *The Rite of Spring* opened Craft's eyes to, and reminded Stravinsky of, aspects of the music's inspirations which had been lost in chromium-plated Western performances: for instance, the dry 'open' bass drum, which 'makes the beginning of the "Danse de la terre" sound like the stampede I.S. says he had in mind'. They met many Soviet musicians, including Shostakovich, Rozhdestvensky, Oistrakh, the pianist Mariya Yudina, as well as Vladimir Rimsky-Korsakov, and of course Stravinsky's own family, his niece Xenia, and her daughter Yelena.

Yet the visit had no consequences. Stravinsky's music was not generally rehabilitated in the USSR for many years afterwards, and he himself seems not to have hankered any more after his homeland. Instead, after concerts in Italy, Venezuela and New York, he returned to Hollywood and resumed work on

*Abraham and Isaac.* The score was completed in March 1963, but not performed until Stravinsky again went to Israel and Craft conducted the piece in Jerusalem and Caesarea in August 1964.

The approach here to biblical narrative could hardly be more different from that in *The Flood.* In place of the picture-book treatment, we now have a cool, abstracted account, by a single voice, tracking syllabically through the text in Hebrew, a language Stravinsky seems to have chosen, not out of deference to the people of the State of Israel (to whom the work was eventually dedicated), but as the ultimate secret sacred language, so secret, in fact, that he himself did not know a word of it and had to be advised by Berlin on the pronunciation and accentuation syllable by syllable. The tone is that of a preacher in the synagogue, lofty but unexcitable, except perhaps at the key passage about 'multiplying thy seed as the stars of heaven'. The texture, essentially decorated monody, varies little; the voice is lightly accompanied almost throughout, and the few moments of thicker chording invariably have an emblematic significance, like the chords framing the episode of the ram in quasi-retrograded rhythm and scoring, which apparently stand for Abraham's obedience and the intervention of God.

*Abraham and Isaac* was to remain Stravinsky's purest and most 'automatic' use of rotations, a fact which has a bearing on the music not least because the numerology clearly refers to the symbolism of the story. Sometimes this is perfectly audible; more often the listener is aware of a patterning process, in the use of intervals, rhythmic figures or even particular words, by which the 12-minute work is being organized and, so to speak, punctuated; sometimes there are symbolisms which can be uncovered by analysis but scarcely detected in performance. The sense of arcane significations tapering away beyond the vanishing-point of direct apprehension certainly seems an authentic part of the musical experience, and an aspect of the work's subtle fascination. But exactly how such things work is, almost by definition, impossible to observe.

Yet another European tour intervened between this and Stravinsky's next work, a set of orchestral variations which Stravinsky, after the novelist's death on 22 November 1963, subtitled 'Aldous Huxley in memoriam'. But on the very same day that Huxley died there was another, more sensational decease, and Stravinsky broke off work on the Variations to compose a short elegy for President Kennedy (whom he had met at a White House dinner in January 1962). The *Elegy for J.F.K.*, completed in March 1964, movingly sets a short poem specially written by Auden ('When a just man dies') for mezzo-soprano or baritone with three clarinets, the same basic scoring as for the *Berceuses du chat*. Stravinsky then returned to the Variations and completed them in August 1964. Where the *Elegy* lasts about a minute and a half, the Variations are three times as long, but still remarkably compressed and, like *Abraham and Isaac*, somewhat arcane. There are 12 variations, but no evident theme, and effectively it is the serial grid that is 'varied'. Every rotation device is deployed: the serial ladder, the stacked chords, even the simultaneous playing of 12 distinct rotations in isorhythm. But as with *The Flood*, what holds the piece together is not any perception this gives of integration, but the sheer speed and energy of the writing itself (which, of course, Stravinsky may have achieved through his own perception of the grid as a unifying device).

This is by no means an elegiac piece; the dedication postdates the conception, and the music is generally buoyant in feeling. By contrast, the *Introitus* which Stravinsky wrote after the death of T.S. Eliot in January 1965 is actually a short setting of the 'Requiem aeternam', and its imagery includes the tocsin idea already used in *A Sermon, a Narrative and a Prayer*, as well as muffled drums and a solemn rhythmic parlando for the choir (male voices) in imitation of the drums. The tocsin figures serve as versets between sections of the text, like the organ interludes in the *Canticum sacrum*. Since many of these devices turn up in the next work, *Requiem Canticles*, there is a distinct sense of the one as a study for the other, or at least of the two belonging together.

Stravinsky was 84 when he completed the *Requiem Canticles* in August 1966, and perhaps it is fitting that his last substantial work should have been a memorial to somebody he did not know personally (Helen Buchanan Seeger) so that the elegiac tone is objectified and returned to the status of ritual which the recent, minimalist tributes had to some extent abandoned (though the sketchbook is nevertheless what Craft has called, in his 'Afterword' to Arnold Newman's *Bravo Stravinsky*, 'a necrology of friends who died during its composition'). The liturgy is admittedly set mainly as a series of headline texts, all from the Proper of the Requiem Mass; only the 'Libera me' is effectively set in full. Most fragmentary of all is the 'Dies irae', only the title words of which are sung, the rest of the first two verses being set as rhythmic speech like the parlando episodes in the *Introitus*; then follow a verse of 'Tuba mirum', two verses of 'Rex tremendae', and the concluding 'Lacrimosa'. Another aspect of the Eliot tribute which Stravinsky adapts for the *Requiem Canticles* is ostinato repetition, a device he had otherwise hardly used since *The Flood*. This serves a kind of antiphony in the prelude (between the pulsing semiquavers of the tutti strings and the gradually expanding dialogue of the concertante group), and in the orchestral interlude, where woodwind polyphonies alternate with phrases of a vestigial funeral march. The 'Libera me' builds up extraordinary emotional intensity by combining chordal chanting with free rhythmic speech – as it were, the multitude of dead souls shadowing the living. Then in the postlude, Stravinsky ends his final masterpiece, as he had ended that much earlier masterpiece about marriage and procreation, with chiming bells: serial bells, indeed, since the four-part chords played by celesta, tubular bells and vibraphone are simply play-throughs of the work's two rows, each in simultaneous prime and inversion.

The *Requiem Canticles* was not the last music Stravinsky wrote. Soon after-wards he composed a simple two-part linear setting for soprano and piano of Lear's *The Owl and the Pussy-Cat*. Then later there were fragmentary sketches for an orchestral work and transcriptions of Wolf and Bach. But while his physical decline continued, there was mercifully no creative decline, merely a cessation. In 1969, the household moved to New York, partly to be closer to the increasingly heavy medical care Stravinsky needed, partly because of a family crisis specific to the West Coast. The following year, indeed, he recovered suffi-ciently to spend part of the summer at Evian, on the French shore of Lake Geneva, and here he was visited by his eldest son Theodore and, from Leningrad, his niece Xenia. In New York the following March there was another brief resur-gence of creative energy, apparently without issue, and at the end of that month, as the final act of a life of travel and exile, he and Vera moved yet again, from the Essex House to an apartment on Fifth Avenue. Here, barely a week later, the composer died (6 April 1971). The funeral was held in New York three days later. However, the body was not interred, but was instead flown to Venice, where, at Vera's wish, it was buried on 14 April, amid considerable pomp, on the cemetery island of San Michele, a few yards from the grave of Sergey Diaghilev.

# 11. THEN AND SINCE

Stravinsky's death removed an artist widely regarded, by 1971, as a figure from the past. Concert audiences were seldom confronted with any work of his from the previous quarter-century, and even in theatrical quarters praise of works later than *The Rite of Spring* was a lot easier to come by than performances. Meanwhile, in modern musical circles his reputation was in the balance. The late serial works, forbidding to lay audiences, were mostly regarded as irrelevant by orthodox avant-garde musicians, while the opposed radical and experimental tendencies rejected them along with the rest of post-Schoenbergian intellectual-ism. What Ernst Roth called the 'special and complex relationship between Stravinsky and the age in which he lived' ('In Remembrance of Igor Stravinsky', *Tempo* no.97, 1971, 6) was certainly not yet generally understood as a consistent, still less as a continuingly active one.

Thirty years later, we can perhaps begin to describe this relationship in more useful terms. Stravinsky's unique artistic trajectory was crucially that of an exile: an exile, moreover, who had been uprooted at the precise moment that he was tapping down most deeply into his native musical soil. And like all productive exiles, he cultivated a flexible and reciprocal association with his changing environment. While consistently producing work that transformed the sensibilities of those who heard it, he himself continuously allowed his own sensibilities to be fed, even transformed, by the music and music-making of others. This is the only plausible explanation of his astonishing ability to absorb other idioms without ever sacrificing the integrity of his own. He himself was well aware of the trait, and made a joke of it. 'I am probably describing a rare form of kleptomania', he told Robert Craft (who himself remarked elsewhere that Stravinsky '*wanted* to be influenced': see *Memories and Commentaries* and 'Influence or Assistance', *Glimpses of a Life*, respectively). Perhaps no great composer has ever had the creative confidence to steal with such energy, and with so little fear that his own personality would be submerged or distorted in the process.

This combination of stylistic diversity and artistic unity and integrity seems now to be the main source of Stravinsky's undimmed vitality as a creative force thirty years after his death. For younger composers of almost every persuasion, his work has continued to offer inspiration and a source of method. And just as he stole without penalty, it seems that at least the best of his successors can go on plundering him with at least the hope of impunity. Essentially a pre-postmodern composer, who exploited the diversity and impersonality of the modern age not in any jaded or dissolute spirit but in order to meet its challenges and survive its menaces, he has emerged as the archetypal prophet of and source for an epoch which now has the doubtful privilege of contemplating those same choices without any comparable threat and at its leisure.

# WORKS

\* excludes some lost and fragmentary works; for details see Goubault (B1991)

Publishers:  Associated [A]; Belyayev [Bel]; Bessell [Bes]; Boosey & Hawkes [B]; Breitkopf & Härtel [Br]; Chappell [Chap]; Charling [Char]; Chester [C]; Faber [F]; Hansen [H]; Henn [He]; Jurgenson [J]; Leeds [L]; Mercury [M]; Edition Russe de Musique [R]; Paul Sacher Stiftung [Sach]; Schott [S]; Sirène [Si]

DRAMATIC

| Title | Genre (acts, libretto/scenario) | Scoring | Composition | First performance | Publication | |
|---|---|---|---|---|---|---|
| Zhar'-ptitsa (L'oiseau de feu) [The Firebird] | fairy tale ballet (2 scenes, M. Fokine) | orch | 1909–10 | cond. G. Pierné, Paris, Opéra, 25 June 1910 | J 1912, S | 9, 10, 11, 12, 23, 27 |
| Petrushka (Pétrouchka) | burlesque (4 scenes, A. Benois) | orch | 1910–11, rev. 1946 | cond. P. Monteux, Paris, Châtelet, 13 June 1911 | R 1912, rev. B 1948 | 10, 11, 13, 15, 18, 23, 27, 32, 46 |
| Vesna svyashchennaya (Le sacre du printemps) [The Rite of Spring (literally 'Sacred Spring')] | scenes of pagan Russia (2 pts, N. Roerich) | orch | 1911–13, Sacrificial Dance, rev. 1943 | cond. Monteux, Paris, Champs-Elysées, 29 May 1913 | R 1913 (for pf 4 hands), R 1921 (full score), rev. Sacrificial Dance A 1945, facs. Sketches B 1969 | 11, 12, 13, 14, 15, 19, 20, 22, 26, 27, 35, 37, 43, 46, 49 |
| Solovey (Le rossignol) [The Nightingale] | musical fairy tale (3, Stravinsky, S. Mitusov after H.C. Andersen) | solo vv, chorus, orch | Act 1, 1908–9; Acts 2–3, 1913–14, rev. | cond. Monteux, Paris, Opéra, 26 May 1914 | R 1923, B, rev. B 1962 | 8, 14, 24 |
| Bayka pro lisu, petukha, kota da barana (Renard) [Fable of the Fox, the Cock, the Tomcat and the Ram/Reynard] | burlesque in song and dance (Stravinsky after A.N. Afanas'yev) | 2 T, 2 B, small orch | 1915–16 | Paris, Opéra, 18 May 1922 | He 1917, C | 16, 21, 27 |
| Svadebka (Les noces) [The Wedding] | Russ. choreographic scenes (4 scenes, Stravinsky after Russ. trad. coll. P.V. Kireyevsky) | S, Mez, T, B, SATB, 4 pf, perc ens | inc. draft, 1914–17; completed 1921–3 | cond. Ansermet, Paris, Gaîté Lyrique, 13 June 1923 | C 1922 (vocal score), C c1923 (full score) | 15, 16, 17, 18, 19, 21, 28, 36, 43 |
| Pesnya solov'ya (Chant du rossignol) [Song of the Nightingale] | sym. poem/ballet (1, Stravinsky after Andersen) [arr. from The Nightingale, acts 2–3] | orch | 1917 | concert perf. cond. E. Ansermet, Geneva, 6 Dec 1919; staged cond. Ansermet, Paris, Opéra, 2 Feb 1920 | R 1921, B | 16, 17, 18 |
| Histoire du soldat | to be read, played and danced (2 pts, C.F. Ramuz) | 3 actors, female dancer, cl, bn, cornet, trbn, perc, vn, db | 1918 | cond. Ansermet, Lausanne, Municipal, 28 Sept 1918 | C 1924 | 15, 17, 21, 22, 28 |
| Pulcinella | ballet with song (1, L. Massine) [after D. Gallo, Pergolesi and others] | S, T, B, chbr orch | 1919–20 | cond. Ansermet, Paris, Opéra, 15 May 1920 | C 1920 (vocal score), R 1924 (full score), B | 18, 19, 23, 26, 41 |
| Mavra | opéra bouffe (1, B. Kochno after A. Pushkin: Domik v Kolomne [The Little House at Kolomna]) | S, Mez, A, T, orch | 1921–2 | cond. G. Fitelberg, Paris, Opéra, 3 June 1922 | R 1925, B | 20, 21, 23, 24, 36 |
| Oedipus rex | op-orat (2, J. Cocteau after Sophocles, Lat. trans. J. Daniélou) | nar, solo vv, male chorus, orch | 1926–7 | concert perf. cond. Stravinsky, Paris, Sarah Bernhardt, 30 May 1927; staged, cond. Wallerstein, Vienna, Staatsoper, 23 Feb 1928 | R 1927 (vocal score), rev. B 1949 | 23, 24, 27, 28, 40, 46 |

| Title | Genre (acts, libretto/scenario) | Scoring | Composition | First performance | Publication | |
|---|---|---|---|---|---|---|
| Apollo (Apollon musagète) | ballet (2 scenes) | str | 1927–8 | cond. H. Kindler, Washington DC, Library of Congress, 27 April 1928 | R 1928, B | 25, 26, 27, 28, 33, 37, 40 |
| Le baiser de la fée | allegorical ballet (4 scenes, Stravinsky after Andersen) [after songs and pf pieces by Tchaikovsky] | orch | 1928 | cond. Stravinsky, Paris, Opéra, 27 Nov 1928 | R 1928, B | 26, 27 |
| Perséphone | melodrama (3 scenes, A. Gide) | spkr, T, SATB, TrA, orch | 1933–4 | cond. Stravinsky, Paris, Opéra, 30 April 1934 | R 1934, B | 29, 31, 32 |
| Jeu de cartes | ballet in 3 deals (Stravinsky, N. Malayev) | orch | 1936 | cond. Stravinsky, New York, Metropolitan, 27 April 1937 | S 1937 | 30, 33 |
| Circus Polka (for a young elephant) | circus band (scored D. Raksin) | | 1942 | cond. M. Evans, New York, Madison Square Gardens, 9 April 1942 | A 1948, S | 35 |
| Scènes de ballet | for revue The Seven Lively Arts | orch | 1944 | cond. M. Abravanel, Philadelphia, Forrest, 24 Nov 1944 | Chap 1945, B | 35, 36 |
| Orpheus | ballet (3 scenes) | orch | 1947 | cond. Stravinsky, New York, City Center, 28 April 1948 | B 1948 | 37, 40, 46 |
| The Rake's Progress | op (3, epilogue, W.H. Auden, C. Kallman) | solo vv, chorus, orch | 1947–51 | cond. Stravinsky, Venice, La Fenice, 11 Sept 1951 | B 1951 | 38, 39, 40 |
| Agon | ballet | orch | 1953–7 | concert perf. cond. R. Craft, Los Angeles, 17 June 1957; staged, cond. R. Irving, New York, City Center, 1 Dec 1957 | B 1957 | 40, 41, 42, 43, 45 |
| The Flood | musical play (Craft after York and Chester mystery plays and Bible: Genesis) | T, 2 B, SAT, actors, nar, orch | 1961–2 | CBS television, broadcast, cond. Stravinsky and Craft, 14 June 1962; staged cond. Craft, Hamburg, Staatsoper, 30 April 1963 | B 1963 | 45, 46, 47, 48 |

ORCHESTRAL

| Title | Scoring | Composition | First performance | Publication | |
|---|---|---|---|---|---|
| Symphony, E♭, op.1 | orch | 1905–7 | movts 2 and 3, cond. H. Wahrlich, St Petersburg, 14/27 April 1907; complete, cond. F. Blumenfeld, St Petersburg, 22 Jan/4 Feb 1908 | J 1914, Forberg | 4, 7, 21 |
| Fantasticheskoye skertso (Scherzo fantastique), op.3 | orch | 1907–8 | cond. A. Ziloti, St Petersburg, 24 Jan/6 Feb 1909 | J 1909, S | 7, 8, 16 |

| Title | Scoring | Composition | First performance | Publication | |
|---|---|---|---|---|---|
| Feyerverk (Feu d'artifice [Fireworks]), op.4 | orch | 1908, rev. 1909 | cond. Ziloti, St Petersburg, 9/22 Jan 1910 | S 1910 | 7, 8, 17, 46 |
| Pogrebal'naya pesn [Funeral Song], op.5 | orch | 1908 | cond. Blumenfeld, St Petersburg, 17/30 Jan 1909 | unpubd, lost | 8 |
| Suite from 'The Firebird' | orch | 1910 | cond. Ziloti, St Petersburg, 23 Oct/5 Nov 1910 | J 1912 | 17, 25 |
| | rev.reduced orch | 1919 | cond. E. Ansermet, Geneva, 12 April 1919 | C 1920 | |
| | rev.reduced orch | 1945 | cond. J. Horenstein, New York, 24 Oct 1945 | L 1946, S | |
| Suite no.2 [arr. of 3 pièces faciles, pf 4 hands, 1914–15, and 5 pièces faciles, pf 4 hands, 1917: no.5] | small orch | 1915–1921 | cond. H. Scherchen, Frankfurt, 25 Nov 1925 | C 1925 | 16 |
| Suite from 'Pulcinella' | chbr orch | 1922 | cond. Monteux, Boston, 22 Dec 1922 | R 1924, B | 43 |
| Concerto | pf, wind, timp, dbs | 1923–4 | Stravinsky, cond. Koussevitzky, Paris, Opéra, 22 May 1924 | R 1924 (2 pf reduction), R 1936 (full score), B | 21, 22 |
| Suite no.1 [arr. of 5 pièces faciles, pf 4 hands, 1917: nos. 1–4] | small orch | 1925 | cond. Stravinsky, Haarlem, 2 March 1926 | C 1926 | |
| Quatre études [arr. of 3 Pieces, str qt, and Study, pianola] | orch | 1928–9 | no.4, cond. Stravinsky, Paris, 16 Nov 1928; complete, cond. Ansermet, Berlin, 7 Nov 1930 | R 1930, B | |
| Capriccio | pf, orch | 1928–9 | Stravinsky, cond. Ansermet, Paris, 6 Dec 1929 | R 1930, B | 27, 28 |
| Violin Concerto, D | | 1931 | S. Dushkin, cond. Stravinsky, Berlin, 23 Oct 1931 | S 1931 | 29 |
| Divertimento [arr. from ballet Le baiser de la fée, 1928] | orch | 1934 | cond. Stravinsky, Paris, 4 Nov 1934 | R 1938, B | |
| Concerto 'Dumbarton Oaks', Eb | chbr orch | 1937–8 | cond. N. Boulanger, Washington DC, 8 May 1938 | S 1938 | 33 |
| Symphony in C | orch | 1938–40 | cond. Stravinsky, Chicago, 7 Nov 1940 | S 1948 | 33, 34, 42 |
| Danses concertantes | chbr orch | 1940–2 | cond. Stravinsky, Los Angeles, 8 Feb 1942 | A 1942, S | 36 |
| Circus Polka | orch | 1942 | cond. Stravinsky, Cambridge, MA, 13 Jan 1944 | A 1942 (pf reduction), 1944, S | 35 |
| Four Norwegian Moods | orch | 1942 | cond. Stravinsky, Cambridge, MA, 13 Jan 1944 | A 1944, S | 35 |
| Ode | orch | 1943 | cond. Koussevitzky, Boston, 8 Oct 1943 | S 1947, A | 35, 36, 46 |
| Symphony in Three Movements | orch | 1942–5 | cond. Stravinsky, New York, 24 Jan 1946 | A 1946, S | 35, 36 |
| Scherzo à la russe [arr. of jazz band piece] | orch | 1945 | cond. Stravinsky, San Francisco, 22 March 1946 | Chap 1945, S | |
| Concerto in D | str | 1946 | cond. P. Sacher, Basle, 27 Jan 1947 | B 1947 | 36 |
| Greeting Prelude [after C.F. Summy: Happy Birthday to you] | orch | 1955 | cond. C. Munch, Boston, 4 April 1955 | B 1956 | |
| Movements | pf, orch | 1958–9 | M. Weber, cond. Stravinsky, New York, 10 Jan 1960 | B 1960 | 44 |
| Monumentum pro Gesualdo di Venosa (ad CD annum) [free arrs. of Gesualdo madrigals] | orch | 1960 | cond. Stravinsky, Venice, 27 Sept 1960 | B 1960 | 44 |
| Variations (Aldous Huxley in memoriam) | orch | 1963–4 | cond. Craft, Chicago, 17 April 1965 | B 1965 | 47 |

Igor Stravinsky in the family
flat at Kryukov Canal 66, St
Petersburg, 1898

Igor Stravinsky in his study at
Ustilug, 1913

Igor Stravinsky and
Ernest Ansermet

Stravinsky (extreme left) and his wife Katya
(extreme right) at the home of Rimsky-Korsakov
(seated next to Stravinsky), together with
Rimsky-Korsakov's daughter Nadezhda and her
fiancé Maximilian Steinberg, St Petersburg, 1908

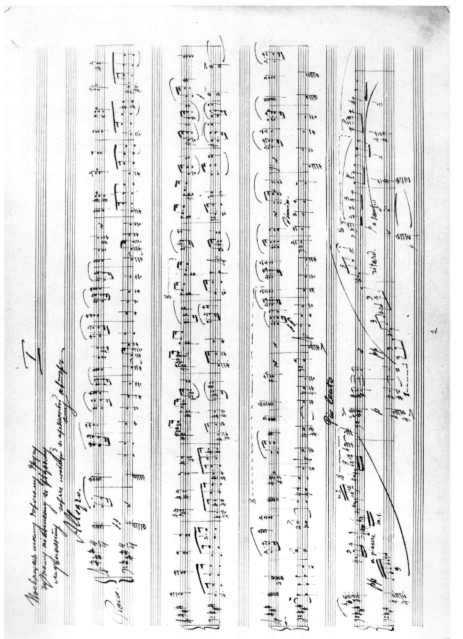

Autograph MS of the beginning of Stravinsky's Piano Sonata in F♯ minor, composed 1903–4 *(RUS-Mcm)*

Sketch by Alexandre Benois for the final scene of Stravinsky's 'Petrushka',
Ballets Russes at the Théâtre du Châtelet, Paris, 1911

Maria Piltz (third from left) as the Chosen One with Russian tribal elders from the first production of Stravinsky's ballet 'The Rite of Spring', Ballets Russes at Théâtre des Champs-Elysées, Paris, 29 May 1913: costume designs by Nikolay Roerich

Stravinsky in conversation with Jean Cocteau

First page of Stravinsky's sketches for 'The Rite of Spring', 1911–13 (*F-Pmeyer*)

Sketch by René Auberjonois for the staging of Stravinsky's 'Histoire du soldat', Lausanne, 1918

Igor Stravinsky: portrait by Pablo Picasso, December 1920

Design by Natal'ya Goncharova, based on the choreography by Bronislava Nizhinska, for Stravinsky's 'The Wedding', Théâtre Gaîté Lyrique, 13 June 1923: pen and black ink heightened with white ink (Victoria and Albert Museum, London)

Page from the autograph MS of Stravinsky's 'Variations (Aldous Huxley in memoriam)', 1963–4 (US-Wc)

Closing scene of Stravinsky's 'Apollo' ('Apollon musagète'), Théâtre Sarah Bernhardt, Paris, 12 June 1928, choreography by Georges Balanchine, designs by André Bauchant, with Serge Lifar as Apollo

Igor Stravinsky, Ostend, 18 November 1931

Igor Stravinsky with his son Soulima and Samuel Dushkin

Stravinsky at an orchestra rehearsal, Teatro La Fenice, Venice, 1951

Stravinsky in his study, December 1952

| Title | Scoring | Composition | First performance | Publication | |
|---|---|---|---|---|---|
| Canon (on a Russian Popular Tune) [theme from finale of The Firebird] | orch | 1965 | cond. Craft, Toronto, 16 Dec 1965 | B 1966 | |

LARGE ENSEMBLE OR BAND

| Title | Scoring | Composition | First performance | Publication | |
|---|---|---|---|---|---|
| March [arr. of 3 pièces faciles, pf 4 hands, 1914–15: no.1] | 12 insts | 1915 | | unpubd | |
| Ragtime | fl, cl, hn, cornet, trbn, perc, cimb, 2 vn, va, db | 1917–18 | cond. A Bliss, London, 27 April 1920 | Si 1920, C | |
| Symphonies d'instruments à vent | 24 insts | 1920; final chorale rev. wind ens without cl, 1945; complete work rev. 1947 for 23 insts | cond. S. Koussevitzky, London, 10 June 1921 | R 1926 (pf reduction), 1945 chorale rev. unpubd; 1947 rev. B 1952 | 18, 19, 20, 28, 36, 37, 41 |
| Praeludium | jazz ens | 1936–7 rev. 1953 | rev. vers:on, cond. Craft, Los Angeles, 18 Oct 1953 | rev. B 1968 | 33 |
| Scherzo à la russe | jazz band | 1943–4 | Paul Whiteman Band, New York (radio), 5 Sept 1944 | A 1946, S | 35 |
| Ebony Concerto | cl, jazz band | 1945 | W. Herman, cond. W. Hendl, New York, 25 March 1946 | Char 1946, Morris | 36 |
| Concertino [arr. of str qt work, 1920] | fl, ob, eng hn, A-cl, 2 bn, 2 tpt, trbn, b trbn, vn, vc | 1952 | cond. Stravinsky, Los Angeles, 11 Nov 1952 | H 1953 | 18, 19 |
| Tango [arr. of pf work, 1940] | 19 insts | 1953 | cond. Craft, Los Angeles, 19 Oct 1953 | M 1954 | 35 |
| Eight Instrumental Miniatures [arr. of Les cinq doigts, pf, 1921] | 15 insts | 1962 | nos.1–4 cond. Craft, Los Angeles, 26 March 1962; nos.1–8 cond. Stravinsky, Toronto, 29 April 1962 | C 1963 | 19 |

CHORAL

| Title, genre | Text | Scoring | Composition | First performance | Publication | |
|---|---|---|---|---|---|---|
| Cantata [for the 60th birthday of Rimsky-Korsakov] | | chorus, ? pf | 1904 | cond. Stravinsky, St Petersburg, 6/19 March 1904 | unpubd, lost | 4, 5 |
| Zvezdolikiy (Le roi des étoiles) [The king of the stars (literally 'Star-Face')] | K. Bal'mont | TTBB, orch | 1911–12 | cond. F. André, Brussels, 19 April 1939 | J 1913 | 11, 12 |

| Title, genre | Text | Scoring | Composition | First performance | Publication | |
|---|---|---|---|---|---|---|
| Podblyudnïye [Saucers (literally 'In the Presence of the Dish'] (Four Russian Peasant Songs) | I. Sakharov | female vv, rev. for equal vv, 4 hn | 1914–17, rev. 1954 | cond. V. Kibalchich, Geneva, 1917; rev. version, Los Angeles, 11 Oct 1954 | S 1930, C, rev. C 1958, S | 15 |
| 1. U spasa v'Chigisakh ['In Our Saviour's Parish at Chigasï'] | | | | | | |
| 2. Ovsen' [Ovsen] | | 4vv | 1916 | | | |
| 3. Shchuka [The Pike] | | 2vv | 1917 | | | |
| 4. Puzishche [Mr Portly] | | 3 solo vv, 4vv | 1914 | | | |
| | | solo v, 4vv | 1915 | | | |
| Otche nash' [Our Father] rev. as Pater noster | Slavonic | SATB | 1926 | Paris, 18 May 1934 | R 1932, B | |
| | Lat. | SATB | 1949 | | B 1949 | |
| Symphonie de psaumes | Pss xxxviii. 13–14, xxxix. 2–4, cl | SATB, orch | 1930 | cond. Ansermet, Brussels, 13 Dec 1930 | R 1930 (vs), R 1931 (fs), B | 27, 28, 33, 38 |
| Simvol verï [Symbol of faith] rev. as Credo | Slavonic | SATB | 1932 | Paris, 18 May 1934 | R 1933, B | |
| | Lat. | SATB | 1949 | | B 1949 | |
| Bogoroditse devo [Blessed Virgin] rev. as Ave Maria | Slavonic | SATB | 1934 | Paris, 18 May 1934 | R 1934 | |
| | Lat. | SATB | 1949 | | B 1949 | |
| Babel, cant. | Genesis xi. 1–9 | male nar, male vv, orch | 1944 | cond. W. Janssen, Los Angeles, 18 Nov 1945 | S 1952 (vs), 1953 (fs) | 35, 46 |
| Mass | Lat. | TrATTB, 2 ob, eng hn, 2 bn, 2 tpt, 3 trbn | 1944–8 | cond. Ansermet, Milan, 27 Oct 1948 | B 1948 | 36 |
| Cantata | late medieval Eng. verse | S, T, female vv, 2 fl, ob, ob + eng hn, vc | 1951–2 | cond. Stravinsky, Los Angeles, 11 Nov 1952 | B 1952 | 39, 40 |
| Canticum sacrum ad honorem Sancti Marci nominis | Vulgate | T, Bar, chorus, orch | 1955 | cond. Stravinsky, Venice, 13 Sept 1956 | B 1956 | 41, 42 |
| Threni: id est Lamentationes Jeremiae prophetae | Vulgate | S, A, 2 T, 2 B, chorus, orch | 1957–8 | cond. Stravinsky, Venice, 23 Sept 1958 | B 1958 | 39, 43, 44, 45 |
| A Sermon, a Narrative and a Prayer, cant. | Bible: Romans viii.24–5, Hebrews xi.1, xii.29; Acts vi–vii; T. Dekker | A, T, spkr, chorus, orch | 1960–61 | cond. Sacher, Basle, 23 Feb 1962 | B 1961 | 45, 48 |
| Anthem 'The dove descending breaks the air' | T.S. Eliot: Little Gidding, pt.IV | SATB | 1962 | cond. Craft, Los Angeles, 19 Feb 1962 | appx. to Expositions and Developments, London, 1962, B | 48 |
| Introitus (T.S. Eliot in memoriam) | Requiem mass (Lat.) | male vv, pf, hp, 2 timp, 2 tam-tams, va, dbs | 1965 | cond. Craft, Chicago, 17 April 1965 | B 1965 | |
| Requiem Canticles | Requiem Mass (Lat.) | A, B, chorus, orch | 1965–6 | cond. Craft, Princeton, 8 Oct 1966 | B 1967 | 48, 49 |

SOLO VOCAL

Tucha [The Storm Cloud] (Pushkin), romance, 1v, pf, 1902 (pubd in *Igor' Stravinsky vokal'naya muzïka*, i, Moscow, 4
1982, F 1986)

Kak gribi na voynu sbiralis' [How the Mushrooms Prepared for War], song, B, pf, 1904 (B 1979)

Konduktor i tarantul [The Driver and the Tarantula] (Koz'ma Prutkov [A.K. Tolstoy, Zhemchuzhnikov brothers]),
1v, pf, 1906, unpubd, lost

Favn' i pastushka (Faune et bergère) [The Faun and the Shepherdess] (song suite, Pushkin), op.2, Mez, orch, 1906 6, 7
(Bel 1908 [vocal score], 1913 [full score], B): 1 Pastushka, 2 Favn', 3 Reka [The River]

Tri pesenki 'Iz vospominaniyha yunosheskikh godov' [Three Little Songs 'Recollections of my Childhood'] (Russ.
trad.), 1v, pf, *c*1906, rev. 1913 (R 1914, B); arr. 1v, small orch, 1929–30 (R 1934, B): 1 Sorochen'ka [The
Magpie], 2 Vorona [The Rook], 3 Chicher' yacher' [The Jackdaw]

Dva romansa (Deux mélodies) (S. Gorodetsky), op.6, Mez, pf, 1907–8 (J *c*1912, B): 1 Vesna (Monastïrskaya) 5, 7
[Spring/The Cloister], 2 Rosyanka (Khlïstovskaya) [A Song of the Dew/Mystic Song of the Ancient Russian
Flagellants]

Pastorale (textless), S, pf, 1907 (J 1910); arr. S, ob, eng hn, cl, bn, 1923 (S) 5, 7

Deux poèmes de Paul Verlaine, op.9, Bar, pf, 1910 (J 1911, B); arr. Bar, chbr orch, 1910, 1951–2 (B 1953): 1 Un 10
grand sommeil noir, 2 La lune blanche

Dva stikhotvoreniya Konstantina Bal'monta [Two Poems of Konstantin Bal'mont], S/T, pf, 1911 (R 1912, B); arr. 11
S/T, 2 fl, 2 cl, pf, str qt, 1954 (B 1955): 1 Nezabudochka tsvetochek' [The Little Forget-Me-Not Flower], 2
Golub' [The Dove]

Tri stikhotvoreniya iz yaponskoy liriki (Trois poésies de la lyrique japonaise) [Three Japanese Lyrics] (trans. A. 12
Brandt), S, pf/(2 fl, 2 cl, pf, str qt), 1912–13 (R 1913, B): 1 Akahito, 2 Mazatsumi, 3 Tsaraiuki; Paris, Salle Erach,
14 Jan 1914

Pribautki (Pribaoutki) (Afanas'yev), male v, pf/(fl, ob + eng hn, cl, bn, vn, va, vc, db), 1914 (He 1917, C): 1 Kornilo, 15
2 Natashka, 3 Polkovnik [The Colonel], 4 Starets i zayats [The Old Man and the Hare]; with pf, Paris, Salle des
Agriculteurs, 20 Nov 1918; with ens, Vienna, Verein für Musikalische Privataufführungen, 6 June 1919

Kolïbel'nïye (Berceuses du chat) [Cat's Cradle Songs] (Russ. trad coll. P. Kireyevsky), A, pf/(E♭-cl, cl + A-cl, A-cl 15
+ b cl), 1915 (He 1917, C): 1 Spi kot [The Tom-Cat], 2 Kot na pechi [The Tom-Cat on the Stove], 3 Bay-bay
[Bye-Byes], 4 U kota, kota [O Tom-Cat, Tom-Cat]; with pf, Paris, Salle des Agriculteurs, 20 Nov 1918; with
ens, Vienna, Verein für Musikalische Privataufführungen, 6 June 1919

Detskiye pesenki (Trois histoires pour enfants) [Three Children's Tales] (P.V. Sheyn, Afanas'yev), 1v, pf, 1916–17 (C 15
1920): 1 Tilimbom, 1917, 2 Gusi-lebedi [Geese, Swans], 1917, 3 Pesenka medvedya [The Bear's Little Song],
1915; no.1 rev. 1v, orch, 1923 (C 1927)

Berceuse (Stravinsky), 1v, pf, 1917 (in Eng. edn of *Expositions and Developments*, London, 1962)

Quatre chants russes (Russ. trad.), 1v, pf, 1918–19 (*La revue romande*, 15 Sept 1919 [nos.3 and 4], C 1920 [com-
plete]): 1 Selezen' (Khorovodnaya) [The Drake/Round], 2 Zapevnaya [Counting Song], 3 Podblyudnaya [Table-
Mat Song], 4 Sektantskaya [Dissident Song]; Paris, Salle Gaveau, 7 Feb 1920; no.4 arr. 1v, fl, cimb, 1918–19 (in
*Stravinsky: Selected Correspondence*, i, London, 1982 [facs.])

Chanson de Paracha, S, orch, 1922–3 (R 1925, B) [arr. from op Mavra, 1921–2]

Petit Ramusianum harmonique (Stravinsky, C.-A. Cingria), 1v/unison vv, 1937 (in *Hommage à C.-F. Ramuz*,
Lausanne, 1938)

Tango (textless), 1v, pf, 1940, unpubd [arr. of pf piece]

Hommage à Nadia Boulanger (Petit canon pour la fête de Nadia Boulanger) (J. de Meung), 2 T, 1947 (B 1982)

Three Songs from William Shakespeare, Mez, fl, cl, va, 1953 (B 1954): 1 Musick to Heare, 2 Full Fadom Five, 3 41
When Dasies Pied; cond. Craft, Los Angeles, 8 March 1954

Four Songs, 1v, fl, hp, gui, 1953–4 (C 1955) [arrs. of 4 chants russes, 1918–19: nos. 1 and 4, and 3 Children's Tales,
1916–17: nos. 2 and 1]: 1 The Drake, 2 A Russian Spiritual, 3 Geese and Swans, 4 Tilimbom

In memoriam Dylan Thomas (Thomas: *Do not go gentle into that good night*), dirge canons and song, T, str qt, 4 trbn, 41
1954 (B 1954); cond. Craft, Los Angeles, 20 Sept 1954

Abraham and Isaac (Bible: *Genesis* xxii, in Heb.), sacred ballad, Bar, chbr orch, 1962–3 (B 1965); cond. Craft, 46, 47
Jerusalem, 23 Aug 1964

Elegy for J.F.K. (Auden), Bar/Mez, 3 cl, 1964 (B 1964); cond. Craft, Los Angeles, 6 April 1964 47

The Owl and the Pussy-Cat (E. Lear), 1v, pf, 1966 (B 1967); P. Bonini, I. Dahl, Los Angeles, 31 Oct 1966 49

CHAMBER AND SOLO INSTRUMENTAL

Three Pieces, str qt, 1914; Paris, 13 May 1915; rev. 1918 (R 1922, B), arr. pf 4 hands (Sach 1994, B) 14

Polka, cimb, 1915 (in *Feuilles musicales* [Lausanne], March–April 1962 [facs.]) [arr. of 3 pièces faciles, pf 4 hands,
1914–15: no.3]

Lied ohne Name, 2 bn, 1916–18 (in *Stravinsky: Selected Correspondence*, i, London, 1982)

Study, pianola, 1917, roll T 967 B (Aeolian Co., 1921); London, Aeolian Hall, 13 Oct 1921; unpubd in score 16

Three Pieces, cl + A-cl, 1918 (C 1920); E. Allegra, Lausanne, Conservatoire, 8 Nov 1919

Suite from 'Histoire du soldat', vn, cl, pf, 1918–19 (C 1920), E. Allegra, J. Porta, J. Iturbi, Lausanne, Conservatoire,
8 Nov 1919; 'grande suite', cl, bn, cornet, trbn, perc, vn, db, 1920 (C 1922), cond. Ansermet, London, Wigmore
Hall, 20 July 1920

Concertino, str qt, 1920 (H 1923); Flonzaley Quartet, New York, 23 Nov 1920 18, 19

Octet, fl, cl, 2 bn, C-tpt, A-tpt, trbn, b trbn, 1922–3 (R 1924, B); cond. Stravinky, Paris Opéra, 18 Oct 1923 21, 23, 28

Suite d'après thèmes, fragments et pièces de Giambattista Pergolesi, vn, pf, 1925 (R 1926, B) [arr. from ballet
Pulcinella, 1919–20]

Berceuse, vn, pf, 1926 (S 1929) [arr. from ballet The Firebird], new version, 1931–2 (S)
Prélude et Ronde des princesses, vn, pf, 1926 (S 1929) [arr. from The Firebird, 1909–10]
Duo concertant, vn, pf, 1931–2 (R 1933, B); Duskin, Stravinsky, Berkin Funkhaus, 28 Oct 1932          29
Chants du rossignol et Marche chinoise, vn, pf, 1932 (R 1934, B) [arr. from op The Nightingale, 1908–14]
Danse russe, vn, pf, 1932 (R 1932 B) [arr. from ballet Petrushka, 1910–11]
Divertimento, vn, pf, 1934 (R 1934, B) [arr. of Divertimento from ballet Le baiser de la fée, 1928]
Scherzo, vn, pf, 1932 (S 1933) [arr. from The Firebird]
Suite italienne, vc, pf, 1932 (R 1934, B) [arr. from ballet Pulcinella, 1919–20]
Suite italienne, vn, pf, 1932 (R 1934, B) [arr. from Pulcinella]          29
Ballade, vn, pf, 1933, collab. Dushkin, unpubd [arr. from ballet Le baiser de la fée, 1928]; new version, 1947, collab. J. Gautier (B 1951)
Pastorale, vn, pf, 1933 (S 1934) [arr. of solo vocal work, 1907]; arr. vn, ob, eng hn, cl, bn, 1933 (S 1934)
Chanson russe, vn, pf, 1937 (R 1938, B) [arr. from op Mavra, 1921–2]; arr. vc, pf (R, B)
Tango, vn, pf, 1940, unpubd [arr. of pf piece, 1940]
Elégie, va/vn, 1944 (Chap 1945, S); G. Prévost, Washington DC, Library of Congress, 26 Jan 1945
Septet, cl, bn, hn, pf, vn, va, vc, 1952–3 (B 1953); cond. Stravinsky, Washington DC, 23 Jan 1954          40
Epitaphium, fl, cl, hp, 1959 (B 1959); Donaueschingen, 17 Oct 1959
Double Canon, str qt, 1959 (B 1960); New York, Town Hall, 20 Dec 1959
Lullaby, tr rec, a rec (B 1960) [arr. from op The Rake's Progress, 1947–51]
Fanfare for a New Theatre, 2 tpt, 1964 (B 1968); R. Nagel, T. Weiss, New York, Linciln Center, 19 April 1964

PIANO

Tarantella, 1898, inc., unpubd          4
Scherzo, g, 1902 (F 1975)          4
Sonata, f♯, 1903–4 (F 1974)          4, 5
[4] Etudes, op.7, 1908 (J 1910)          8
Valse des fleurs, pf 4 hands, 1914 (in R. Craft: *A Stravinsky Scrapbook 1940–1971*, London, 1983 [facs.])
Trois pièces faciles, 4 hands, 1914–15 (He 1917, C): 1 Marche, 2 Valse, 3 Polka; J. Meerovitch, A. Casella, Paris, 9          16
   Feb 1918
Souvenir d'une marche boche, 1915 (in E. Wharton, ed.: *The Book of the Homeless*, London, 1916)
Cinq pièces faciles, 4 hands, 1917 (He 1917, C): 1 Andante, 2 Española, 3 Balalaika, 4 Napolitana, 5 Galop;
   Meerovitch, Casella, paris, 9 Feb 1918
Valse pour les enfants, 1916 or 1917 (in *Le figaro*, 21 May 1922)
Ragtime, 1917–18 (C 1920) [arr. of work for 11 insts]
Piano-Rag-Music, 1919 (C 1920)l J. Iturbi, Lausanne, Conservatoire, 9 Nov 1919          17
Concertino, 4 hands ?1920 (H 1923) [arr. of str qt piece]
Les cinq doigts, 1921 (C 1922); J. Wiéner, Paris, Salle des Agriculteurs, 15 Dec 1921          19
Three Movements from 'Petrushka', 1921 (R 1922, B) [from ballet, 1910–11]          32
Sonata, 1924 (R 1925, B); F. Petyrek, Donaueschingen, 16 July 1925          22, 23
Serenade in A, 1925 (R 1926, B); I. Stravinsky, Frankfurt, 24 Nov 1925          22, 23
Concerto, 2 pf, 1932–5 (S 1936); S. and I. Stravinsky, Paris, Salle Gaveau, 21 Nov 1935          29, 30, 32
Tango, 1940 (M 1941)          35
Circus Polka, 1941–2 (A c1942)          35
Sonata, 2 pf, 1943–4 (Chap 1945, S); N. Boulanger, R. Johnston, Madison, WI, Edgewood College, 2 Aug 1944          36

REDUCTIONS OF WORKS

by (or apparently by) the composer

*Arrangements certainly or apparently intended as independent works are listed above; the following published reductions by the composer were made for rehearsal or amateur use.*

Vocal scores: The Faun and the Shepherdess, The King of the Stars, The Nightingale, Bayka (Reynard), Pulcinella, Mavra, The Wedding, Oedipus rex, Babel, Cantata, Three Songs from William Shakespeare, In memoriam Dylan Thomas, Canticum sacrum
Pf solo: The Firebird, Song of the Nightingale, Histoire du soldat, Apollo, Le baiser de la fée, Jeu de cartes, Praeludium
Pf 4 hands: Petrushka, The Rite of Spring
2 pf: Concerto for pf and wind, Capriccio, Concerto 'Dumbarton Oaks', Septet, Agon, Movements
Vn, pf; Violin Concerto

ARRANGEMENTS

F. Chopin: Nocturne, A♭, op.32/2; Valse brillante, E♭, op.18, orch, 1909, unpubd [for ballet Les sylphides]          9
Two 'Songs of the Flea' (J.W. von Goethe), B, orch, 1909 (no.1, Bes, c1923, B; no.2, B) [arr. of Musorgsky and          8
   Beethoven: op.75/3]
E. Grieg: Kobold, op.71, no.3, 1910, unpubd, lost [later used in ballet Les orientales]          9

M. Musorgsky: final chorus and aria of Khovanshchina, 1913, remainder arr. Ravel; unpubd except for vocal score   12, 13, 14
    of Stravinsky's final chorus, based on theme by Musorgsky (Bes 1914)     17

Song of the Volga Boatmen, wind, perc., 1917 (C 1920)

M. Musorgsky: Boris Godunov: chorus 'Na kogo tï nas pokidayesh'' (Prologue), pf, 1918, unpubd

R. de Lisle: La marseillaise, vn, 1919, unpubd

P. Tchaikovsky: The Sleeping Beauty: Variation d'Aurore (Act 2, no.16b); Entr'acte (Act 2, no.19), orch, 1921,
    unpubd

P. Tchaikovsky: The Sleeping Beauty: Bluebird Pas-de-deux (Act 3, nos.10–13), small orch, 1941 (S 1953, B)

The Star-Spangled Banner, orch, 1941 (M)

J.S. Bach: Choral-Variationen über das Weihnachtslied 'Vom Himmel hoch da komm' ich her', chorus, orch, 1955–6   41
    (B 1956)

C. Gesualdo di Venosa: Tres sacrae cantiones, sextus and bassus parts supplied, 1957–9 (B 1957 [no.3], B 1960   44
    [complete]): 1 Da pacem Domine, 2 Assumpta est Maria, 3 Illumina nos

J. Sibelius: Canzonetta, op. 62a, 2 cl, 4 hn, hp, db, 1963 (Br 1964)

H. Wolf: Two Sacred Songs: Herr, was trägt der Boden hier, Wunden trägst du, from the Spanisches Liederbuch,   49
    Mez, 10 insts, 1968 (B 1969)

J.S. Bach: Four Preludes and Fugues from Das wohltemperirte Clavier: bk 1, c♯, e, b; bk 2, d), str, ww, 1969,   47
    unpubd

Mss in *CH-Bps*, *F-Pn*, *GB-Lbl*, *US-Wcg*; for Further locations of individual autographs see Goubault (1991)

# WRITINGS

This list omits interviews, programme notes, letters to newspaper editors, and later articles, many of them reprinted in *Themes and Conclusions* (1972); the authenticity of much of this later material may be regarded as questionable.

Many of the articles in this list are reprinted in E.W. White: *Stravinsky: the Composer and his Works* (London, 2/1979) [SCW].

'Ce que j'ai voulu exprimer dans "Le sacre du printemps"', *Montjoie!* (29 May 1913); repr. in *Igor Stravinsky: Le sacre du printemps: dossier de presse*, ed. F. Lesure (Geneva, 1980), 13–15; Eng. trans. in *Boston Evening Transcript* (12 Feb 1916); repr. in V. Stravinsky and R. Craft: *Stravinsky in Pictures and Documents* (London and New York, 1978), 524–6 [apparently written up from an interview by R. Canudo]

'Les Espagnols aux Ballets Russes', *Comoedia* (15 May 1921); repr. in *Stravinsky: études & témoignages*, ed. F. Lesure (Paris, 1982), 238

'The Genius of Tchaikovsky', *The Times* (18 Oct 1921); repr. in *SCW*, 573–4 [open letter to Diaghilev]

'Une lettre de Stravinsky sur Tchaikovsky', *Le Figaro* (18 May 1922); repr. in *ReM*, iii/9–10 (1921–2)

'Some Ideas about my Octuor', *The Arts* [Brooklyn, NY] (1924), Jan, 4–6; repr. in *SCW*, 574–7

'Avertissement … a Warning', *The Dominant* [London] (1927), Dec, 13–14; repr. in *SCW*, 577–8

'Igor Strawinsky nous parle de "Perséphone"', *Excelsior* (29 April 1934); repr. with corrections in *Excelsior* (1 May 1934); repr. in *SCW*, 579–81

'Quelques confidences sur la musique', *Conferencia* (15 Dec 1935); repr. in *SCW*, 581–5

with W. Nouvel: *Chroniques de ma vie* (Paris, 1935–6; Eng. trans., 1936, as *An Autobiography*)

'Ma candidature à l'Institut', *Jour* (28 Jan 1936); repr. in *Stravinsky: études & témoignages*, ed. F. Lesure (Paris, 1982), 255–7; Eng. trans. in V. Stravinsky and R. Craft: *Stravinsky in Pictures and Documents* (London and New York, 1978), 342–3

*Pushkin: Poetry and Music* (New York, 1940); repr. in *SCW*, 588–91

with Roland-Manuel and P. Souvtchinsky: *Poétique musicale* (Cambridge, MA, 1942; Eng. trans., 1947, as *Poetics of Music*)

with W. Nouvel: 'The Diaghilev I Knew', *Atlantic Monthly* (1953), Nov, 33–6

with R. Craft: *Conversations with Igor Stravinsky* (New York and London, 1959) [early inc. versions: '35 Antworten auf 35 Fragen', *Melos*, xxiv (1957), 161–70; 'Answers to 34 Questions: an Interview with Igor Stravinsky', *Encounter*, ix/sol;7 (1957), 3–14; 'Entretiens d'Igor Stravinsky avec Robert Craft', *Avec Stravinsky* (Monaco, 1958)]

with R. Craft: *Memories and Commentaries* (New York and London, 1960)

with R. Craft: *Expositions and Developments* (New York and London, 1962)

with R. Craft: *Dialogues and a Diary* (Garden City, NY, 1963, enlarged 1968)

with R. Craft: *Themes and Episodes* (New York, 1966, 2/1967)

with R. Craft: *Retrospectives and Conclusions* (New York, 1969)

*Themes and Conclusions* (London, 1972) [combined repr. of *Themes and Episodes* and *Retrospectives and Conclusions*]

# BIBLIOGRAPHY

A: Correspondence. B: Catalogues and bibliographies. C: Facsimiles. D: Life and works. E: Collections of essays. F: Memoirs. G: Further biographical. H: Critical evaluations. I: Analytical studies. J: Ballets. K: Operas. L: Other dramatic works. M: Orchestral and large ensemble works. N: Vocal and choral works. O: Chamber and solo instrumental works. P: Arrangements. Q: Iconography. R: Reception history.

## A: Correspondence

C.F. Ramuz: *Lettres, 1900–1918* (Lausanne, 1956)

C.F. Ramuz: *Lettres, 1919–1947* (Etoy, 1959)

I.Ya. Vershinina, ed.: 'Pis'ma I. Stravinskogo N. Rerikhu' [Letters from Stravinsky to Roerich], *SovM* (1966), no.8, pp.57–63

G. Guisan, ed.: *C.F. Ramuz, ses amis et son temps* (Lausanne and Paris, 1967)

H. de Wendel, ed.: *Francis Poulenc: Correspondance 1915–1963* (Paris, 1967, enlarged 2/1994, ed. M. Chimènes; Eng. trans., enlarged, 1991, as *Francis Poulenc: Echo and Source*)

L. Dyachkova, ed.: *I.F. Stravinsky: stat'i i materialï* [Articles and materials] (Moscow, 1973)

M. Goldstein: 'Zwei Briefe von Igor Strawinsky (Erstveröffentlichung)', *Musik des Ostens*, vii (1975), 280–83

N. Kinkul'kina, ed.: 'Pis'ma I.F. Stravinskogo i F.I. Shalyapina k A.A. Saninu' [Letters from Stravinsky and Chaliapin to Sanin], *SovM* (1978), no.6, pp.92–6

P. Sulzer, ed.: *Zehn Komponisten um Werner Reinhart* (Winterthur, 1979–83)

F. Lesure, ed.: *Claude Debussy: Lettres 1884–1918* (Paris, 1980; enlarged 1993, as *Claude Debussy: Correspondance 1884–1918*; Eng. trans., 1987)

R. Craft, ed.: *Stravinsky: Selected Correspondence* (London and New York, 1982–5)

R. Craft and L. Davidova, eds.: *Dearest Bubushkin: the Correspondence of Vera and Igor Stravinsky, 1921–1954, with Excerpts from Vera Stravinsky's Diaries, 1922–1971* (London, 1985)

N. Rodriguez and M.H. Brown: 'Prokofiev's Correspondence with Stravinsky and Shostakovich', *Slavonic and Western Music: Essays for Gerald Abraham*, ed. M.H. Brown and R.J. Wiley (Ann Arbor and Oxford, 1985)

A. Orenstein: *Maurice Ravel: lettres, écrits et entretiens* (Paris, 1989; Eng. trans., 1990, as *A Ravel Reader: Correspondence, Articles, Interviews*)

C. Tappolet, ed.: *Correspondance Ansermet–Stravinsky (1914–1967)* (Geneva, 1990–92)

*MAk* (1992), no.4 [Stravinsky issue; incl. many early letters]

P. Collaer: *Correspondance avec des amis musiciens* (Sprimont, 1996)

V. Varunts, ed.: *Perepiska s russkimi korrespondentami: materialï k biografii* [Russian correspondence: material for a biography] (Moscow, 1997–)

## B: Catalogues and bibliographies

*Stravinsky and the Dance: a Survey of Ballet Productions, 1910–1962* (New York, 1962)

*Stravinsky and the Theatre: a Catalogue of Decor and Costume Designs for Stage Productions of his Works* (New York, 1963)

K. Thompson: *A Dictionary of Twentieth Century Composers* (London, 1973) [incl. comprehensive bibliography up to 1971]

D.-R. de Lerma and T.J. Ahrens, eds.: *Igor Fedorovitch Stravinsky: a Practical Guide to Publications of his Music* (Kent, OH, 1974)

F. Lesure, ed.: *Igor Stravinsky: la carrière européenne*, Musée d'art moderne, Paris, 14 Oct–30 Nov 1980 (Paris, 1980) [exhibition catalogue]

C. Caesar: *Igor Stravinsky: a Complete Catalogue* (San Francisco, 1982)

R. Craft: 'Selected Source Material from "A Catalogue of Books and Music Inscribed to and/or Autographed and Annotated by Igor Stravinsky"', *Confronting Stravinsky*, ed. J. Pasler (San Diego, 1982), 349–57

C.M. Joseph: 'Stravinsky Manuscripts in the Pierpont Morgan Library and the Library of Congress', *JM*, i (1982), 327–37

A. Schouvaloff and V. Borovsky: *Stravinsky on Stage* (London, 1982)

J. Shepard: 'The Stravinsky *Nachlass*: a Provisional Checklist of Music Manuscripts', *Notes*, xl (1983–4), 719–50

*Strawinsky: sein Nachlass, sein Bild*, Kunstmuseum, Basle, 6 Jun–9 Sept 1984 (Basle, 1984) [exhibition catalogue]

J.R. Heintze: *Igor Stravinsky: an International Bibliography of Theses and Dissertations, 1925–87* (Warren, MI, 1988)

H.J. Jans and L. Handschin, eds.: *Igor Stravinsky: Musikmanuskripte* (Winterthur, 1989)

C. Goubault: *Igor Stravinsky* (Paris, 1991) [catalogue and chronology]

P. Stuart: *Igor Stravinsky: the Composer in the Recording Studio* (New York, 1991) [discography]

H. Lindlar: *Lubbes Strawinsky-Lexikon* (Bergisch-Gladbach, 1994)

F. Meyer, ed.: *Settling New Scores: Music Manuscripts from the Paul Sacher Foundation* (Mainz, 1998)

## C: Facsimiles

I. Stravinsky and R. Craft: *The Rite of Spring: Sketches 1911–1913* (London, 1969)

L. Cyr, ed.: *L'oiseau de feu: facsimile du manuscrit* (Geneva, 1985)

A.I. Klimovitsky: 'Dve "Pesnio Blokhe" – Bětkovena i Musorgskogo – v instrumentovke Stravinskogo' ['Two "Songs of the Flea" – by Beethoven and Musorgsky – in the orchestration of Stravinsky'], *Pamyatniki kul'turï: norïye otkritiya 1984* (Leningrad, 1986), 196–216

A. Baltensperger and F. Meyer, eds.: *Igor Stravinsky: Symphonies d'instruments à vent: Faksimileausgabe des Particells und der Partitur der Erstfassung (1920)* (Basle and Winterthur, 1991)

H. Danuser, F. Meyer and U. Mosch, eds.: *Trois pièces pour quatuor à cordes: Skizzen, Fassungen, Dokumente, Essays: Festgabe für Albi Rosenthal* (Basle and Winterthur, 1994)

## D: Life and works

A. Schaeffner: *Strawinsky* (Paris, 1931)

A. Tansmann: *Igor Stravinsky* (Paris, 1948; Eng. trans., 1949, as *Igor Stravinsky: the Man and his Music*)

H. Kirchmeyer: *Igor Stravinsky: Zeitgeschichte im Persönlichkeitsbild* (Regensburg, 1958)

R. Vlad: *Strawinsky* (Rome, 1958, 2/1973; Eng. trans., 1960, enlarged 3/1979)

R. Siohan: *Stravinsky* (Paris, 1959, 2/1971; Eng. trans., 1965)

B. Yarustovsky: *Igor Stravinsky: kratkiy ocherk zhizni i tvorchestva* [A short study of his life and works] (Moscow, 1963, enlarged 2/1969, 3/1982; Ger. trans., 1966)

N. Nabokov: *Igor Stravinsky* (Berlin, 1964)

E.W. White: *Stravinsky: the Composer and his Works* (London, 1966, enlarged 2/1979)

V.V. Smirnov: *Tvorcheskoye formirovaniye I.F. Stravinskogo* [Stravinsky's creative process] (Leningrad, 1970)

M. Druskin: *Igor' Stravinsky: lichnost', tvorchestvo, vzglyadï* (Leningrad, 1974, enlarged 2/1979; Eng. trans., 1983, as *Igor Stravinsky: his Personality, Works and Views*)

L. Erhardt: *Igor Strawiński* (Warsaw, 1978)

V. Stravinsky and R. Craft: *Stravinsky in Pictures and Documents* (London and New York, 1978)

A. Boucourechliev: *Igor Stravinsky* (Paris, 1982; Eng. trans., 1987)

W. Burde: *Stravinsky: Leben, Werke, Dokumente* (Mainz, 1982, enlarged 2/1992)

V. Scherliess: *Igor Strawinsky und seine Zeit* (Laaber, 1983)

S. Walsh: *The Music of Stravinsky* (London, 1988)

P. Griffiths: *Stravinsky* (London, 1992)

M. Oliver: *Igor Stravinsky* (London, 1995)

R. Taruskin: *Stravinsky and the Russian Traditions* (Berkeley and Oxford, 1996)

S. Walsh: *Stravinsky: A Creative Spring* (New York and London, 1999–2000)

# E: Collections of essays

*ReM*, V/1–2 (1923–4) [Stravinsky Issue]

M. Armitage, ed.: *Igor Stravinsky* (New York, 1936)

*ReM*, no.191 (1939) [Stravinsky issue]

*Tempo*, no.8 (1948) [Stravinsky issue]

E. Corle, ed.: *Igor Stravinsky* (New York, 1949)

*The Score*, no.20 (1957) [Stravinsky issue]

R. Craft, ed.: *Avec Stravinsky* (Monaco, 1958)

*MQ*, xlviii/3 (1962) [Stravinsky issue]; repr. as *Stravinsky: a New Appraisal of his Work*, ed. P.H. Lang (New York, 1963)

B. Boretz and E.T. Cone, eds.: *Perspectives on Schoenberg and Stravinsky* (Princeton, NJ, 1968, 2/1972)

*PNM*, ix/2–x/1 (1971) [Stravinsky issue]

*Tempo*, no.97 (1971) [Stravinsky issue]

R. Craft: *Prejudices in Disguise* (New York, 1974)

J. Pasler, ed.: *Confronting Stravinsky* (San Diego, 1982)

F. Lesure, ed.: *Stravinsky: études & témoignages* (Paris, 1982)

C.J. Oja, ed.: *Stravinsky in 'Modern Music', 1924–1946* (New York, 1982)

*Igor Strawinsky*, Musik-Konzepte, nos.34–5 (1984)

R. Craft: *Present Perspectives* (New York, 1984)

G.S. Alfeyevskaya and I.Ya. Vershinina, eds.: *I.F. Stravinsky: stat'i, vospominaniya* [Articles and reminiscences] (Moscow, 1985)

E. Haimo and P. Johnson, eds.: *Stravinsky Retrospectives* (Lincoln, NE, 1987)

R. Craft: *Small Craft Advisories* (London, 1989)

R. Craft: *Stravinsky: Glimpses of a Life* (New York and London, 1992–3)

R. Craft: *The Moment of Existence* (Nashville, TN and London, 1996)

V. Varunts, ed.: *I.F. Stravinsky: Sbornik statey* [Collection of articles] (Moscow, 1997)


## F: Memoirs

J. Cocteau: 'Stravinsky dernière heure', *ReM*, V/1–2 (1923–4), 142–4

C.F. Ramuz: *Souvenirs sur Igor Strawinsky* (Paris, 1929, 3/1952)

H. Strobel: 'Strawinsky privat', *Melos*, x (1931), 315–18

L. Kirstein: 'Working with Stravinsky', *MM*, xiv (1936–7), 143–6; repr. in *Stravinsky in 'Modern Music', 1924–1946*, ed. C.J. Oja (New York, 1982), 153–7

A. Benois: *Reminiscences of the Russian Ballet* (London, 1941)

W. Tappolet: 'Strawinsky en Suisse Romande', *SMz*, lxxxii (1942), 145–8, 172–7

G. Antheil: *Bad Boy of Music* (London, 1945)

E. de Polignac: 'Memoirs of the Late Princesse Edmond de Polignac', *Horizon* (1945), Aug, 110–41

T. Karsavina: 'A Recollection of Strawinsky', *Tempo*, no.8 (1948), 7–9

S. Dushkin: 'Working with Stravinsky', *Igor Stravinsky*, ed. E. Corle (New York, 1949), 179–92

R. Rolland: *Journal des années de guerre, 1914–1919* (Paris, 1952)

H. Raynor: 'Stravinsky the Teacher', *The Chesterian*, xxxi (1956–7), 35–41, 69–75

R. Craft: 'A Personal Preface', *The Score*, no.20 (1957), 7–13

M. Perrin: 'Stravinsky in a Composition Class', ibid., 44–6

V.V. Yastrebstev: *N.A. Rimsky-Korsakov: vospominaniya 1886–1908* [Reminiscences], ed. A.V. Ossovsky (Leningrad, 1959–60; abridged Eng. trans., 1985, as *Reminiscences of Rimsky-Korsakov*)

W.H. Auden: 'Craftsman, Artist, Genius', *The Observer* (11 April 1971)

R. Craft: *Stravinsky: Chronicle of a Friendship, 1948–1971* (New York and London, 1972, enlarged 2/1994)

P. Horgan: *Encounters with Stravinsky: a Personal Record* (New York and London, 1972, 2/1989)

L. Kutateladze and A. Gozenpud, eds.: *F. Stravinsky: stat'i, pis'ma, vospominaniya* [Articles, letters, reminiscences] (Leningrad, 1972)

L. Libman: *And Music at the Close: Stravinsky's Last Years: a Personal Memoir* (New York, 1972)

N. Nabokov: *Bagazh* (New York, 1975)

L. Morton: 'Stravinsky at Home', *Confronting Stravinsky*, ed. J. Pasler (San Diego, 1982) 332–48

V. Varunts, ed.: *I. Stravinsky, publitsist i sobesednik* [Publicist and interviewee] (Moscow, 1988)


## G: Further biographical

P. Hostowiec [J. Stempowski]: 'Dom Strawinskiego W Uscilugu' [Stravinsky's House At Ustilug], *kultura* (Paris, 1949), 19–34; Repr. In J. Stempowski: *w doline Dniestru I inne eseje ukraińskie* (Warsaw, 1993), 49–77

R. Craft: 'The Composer and the Phonograph', *High Fidelity*, vii (1959), 35

P. Meylan: *Une amitié célèbre: C.F. Ramuz–Igor Stravinsky* (Lausanne, 1962)

K.Yu. Stravinskaya: 'Iz semeynogo arkhiva Stravinskikh' [From the Stravinsky family archives], *SovM* (1970), no.9, pp.154–6

E.W. White: 'Stravinsky in Interview', *Tempo*, no.97 (1971), 6–9

G. Pestelli: *Il giovane Stravinski (1906–1913)* (Turin, 1973)

F. Auberjonois: 'The Swiss Years of Igor Stravinsky', *Adam International Review*, xxxix (1973–4), 73–80

K.Yu. Stravinskaya: *O I.F. Stravinskom i ego blizkikh* [On Stravinsky and his relations] (Leningrad, 1978)

A. Gold and R. Fizdale: *Misia* (New York, 1980) [biography of Misia Sert]

E. Allen: 'The Genius and the Goddess', *Confronting Stravinsky*, ed. J. Pasler (San Diego, 1982), 327–31

M.H. Brown: 'Stravinsky and Prokofiev: Sizing up the Competition', ibid., 39–50

R. Lawson: 'Stravinsky and the Pianola', ibid., 284–301

J. Pasler: 'Stravinsky and the Apaches', *MT*, cxxiii (1982), 403–5

B. Schwarz: 'Stravinsky, Dushkin, and the Violin', *Confronting Stravinsky*, ed J. Pasler (San Diego, 1982), 302–9

L. Stein: 'Schoenberg and "Kleine Modernsky"', ibid., 310–24

I.S. Zil'bershteyn and V.A. Samkov, eds.: *Sergey Dyagilev i russkoye iskusstvo* [Diaghilev and Russian art] (Moscow, 1982)

H. Sachs: *Music in Fascist Italy* (London, 1987)

W.H. Rosar: 'Stravinsky and MGM', *Film Music*, i (1989), 108–22

N. Röthlin: 'Strawinskys juristische Ausbildung', *Quellenstudien I*, ed. H. Oesch (Basle, 1991), 33–51

J. Aguila: *Le domaine musical: Pierre Boulez et vingt ans de création contemporaine* (Paris, 1992)

A. Baltensperger: 'Strawinskys "Chicago Lecture" (1944)', *Mitteilungen der Paul Sacher Stiftung*, v (1992), 19–23

J. Evans: *Hans Rosbaud: a Bio-Bibliography* (New York, 1992)

S. Savenko: 'Na Rodinu v gosti ...' [To the Homeland as a guest], *MAk* (1992), no.4, pp.214–22

V. Varunts: 'Kommentariy k marginaliyam: Shonberga o Stravinskom' [A commentary on marginalia: of Schoenberg about Stravinsky], ibid., 182–4

C.M. Joseph: 'Stravinsky on Film', *Mitteilungen der Paul Sacher Stiftung*, vi (1993), 30–34

V. Varuntz [Varunts]: 'Strawinsky protestiert ...', ibid., 35–7

## H: Critical evaluations

M.D. Calvocoressi: 'A Russian Composer of Today', *MT*, lii (1911), 511–12

E. Vuillermoz: 'Igor Stravinsky', *BSIM*, viii/5 (1912), 15–21

C. van Vechten: *Music after the Great War* (New York, 1915)

C.S. Wise: 'Impressions of Igor Stravinsky', *MQ*, ii (1916), 249–56

E. Ansermet: 'L'oeuvre d'Igor Strawinsky', *ReM*, ii/9–11 (1921), 1–27

B. de Schloezer: 'Igor Stravinsky', *ReM*, v/1–2 (1923–4), 97–141

B. de Schloezer: 'Igor Stravinsky and Serge Prokofjeff', *Melos*, iv (1924–5), 469–81

N. Boulanger: *Lectures on Modern Music* (Houston, 1926)

A. Casella: *Igor Strawinski* (Rome, 1926)

A. Lourié: 'Muzïka Stravinskogo', *Vyorstï*, i (1926), 119–35

L. Sabaneyev: *Modern Russian Composers* (New York, 1927)

A. Lourié: 'Neogothic and Neoclassic', *MM*, v/3 (1927–8), 3–8

L. Laloy: *La musique retrouvée* (Paris, 1928)

B. de Schloezer: 'Igor Stravinsky', *The Dial*, lxxxv (1928), 271–38; lxxxvi (1929), 105–15, 298–303, 463–74

B. de Schloezer: 'Sur Strawinsky', *ReM*, x/4–5 (1928–9), 1–19

P. Landormy: 'L'art russe et Igor Stravinsky', *Musique*, ii (1929), 933–9, 999–1003

B. de Schloezer: *Igor Stravinsky* (Paris, 1929)

P. Collaer: *Strawinsky* (Brussels, 1930)

E.W. White: *Stravinsky's Sacrifice to Apollo* (London, 1930)

D. de' Paoli: *L'opera di Strawinsky* (Milan, 1931, rev., enlarged 1934 as *Igor Strawinsky: da 'L'oiseau de feu' a 'Persefone'*)

H. Fleischer: *Strawinsky* (Berlin, 1931)

J. Handschin: *Igor Strawinski: Versuch einer Einführung* (Zürich, 1933); repr. in *Strawinsky: sein Nachlass, sein Bild* (Basle, 1984)

M. Blitzstein: 'The Phenomenon of Stravinsky', *MQ*, xxi (1935), 330–47

A. Schaeffner: 'Le "purisme" d'Igor Stravinsky', *Europe: revue mensuelle*, xliv (1937), 184–202

S. Lifar: 'Igor Strawinsky: législateur au ballet', *ReM*, nos.188–91 (1939), 321–30

Roland-Manuel: 'Démarche de Strawinsky', ibid., 255–60

A. Schaeffner: 'Critique et thématique', ibid., 241–54

A. Kall: 'Stravinsky in the Chair of Poetry', *MQ*, xxvi (1940), 283–96

N. Nabokov: 'Stravinsky Now', *Partisan Review*, xi (1944), 324–34

A. Salazar: *La musica moderna* (Buenos Aires, 1944; Eng. trans., 1946, as *Music in Our Time*)

G.F. Malipiero: *Strawinsky* (Venice, 1945)

R. Leibowitz: 'Igor Stravinsky, ou Le choix de la misère musicale', *Temps modernes*, i (1946), 1320–36

P. Souvtchinsky: 'Igor Stravinsky', *Contrepoints*, no.2 (1946), 19–31

A. Casella: *Strawinski* (Brescia, 1947; rev. 2/1951)

E.W. White: *Stravinsky: a Critical Survey* (London, 1947)

R. Leibowitz: 'Schönberg and Stravinsky', *Partisan Review*, xv (1948), 361–5

T. Strawinsky: *Le message d'Igor Strawinsky* (Lausanne, 1948; Eng. trans., 1953)

T.W. Adorno: *Philosophie der neuen Musik* (Tübingen, 1949, 3/1967; Eng. trans., 1973)

N. Nabokov: 'Igor Stravinsky', *Atlantic Monthly*, no.184 (1949), 21–7

C. Stuart: 'Stravinsky: the Dialectics of Dislike', *Music-Survey*, ii (1949–50), 142–8

N. Cazden: 'Humor in the Music of Stravinsky and Prokofiev', *Science and Society*, xviii (1954), 52–74

H. Keller: 'Schönberg and Stravinsky: Schönbergians and Stravinskians', *MR*, xv (1954), 307–10

M. Mann: 'Reaction and Continuity in Musical Composition', ibid., 39–46 [review of T.W. Adorno: *Philosophie der neuen Musik* (Tübingen, 1949)]

A. Berger: 'Stravinsky and the Younger American Composers', *The Score*, no.12 (1955), 38–46

H. Strobel: *Stravinsky: Classic Humanist* (New York, 1955; Ger. orig., 1956, as *Igor Strawinsky*)

F. Burt: 'An Antithesis', *The Score*, no.18 (1956), 35–51

W. Schuh: 'Strawinsky und die Tradition', *Melos*, xxiii (1956), 308–13

R. Sessions: 'Thoughts on Stravinsky', *The Score*, no.20 (1957), 32–7

H.H. Stuckenschmidt: *Strawinsky und sein Jahrhundert* (Berlin, 1957)

P. Souvtchinsky: 'Qui est Strawinsky?', *Cahiers musicaux*, iii/16 (1958), 7–14

E. Ansermet: *Les fondements de la musique dans la conscience humaine* (Neuchâtel, 1961)

J. Noble: 'Debussy and Stravinsky', *MT*, cviii (1967), 22–4

S. Karlinsky: 'Igor Stravinskii, East and West', *Slavic Review*, xxvii (1968), 452–8

E. Ansermet: *Ecrits sur la musique* (Neuchâtel, 1971)

C. Spies: 'Impressions after an Exhibition', *Tempo*, no.102 (1972), 2–9

R. Middleton: 'Stravinsky's Development: a Jungian Approach', *ML*, liv (1973), 289–301

V. Smirnov: 'Tvorcheskaya vesna Igorya Stravinskogo' [The creative spring of Igor Stravinsky], *Rasskazi o muzike i muzikantakh*, ed. M.G. Aranovsky (Leningrad, 1973), 55–79

S. Karlinsky: 'The Repatriation of Igor Stravinsky', *Slavic Review*, xxxiii (1974), 528–32

A. Schoenberg: 'Igor Stravinsky: *Der Restaurateur*', 'Stravinsky's *Oedipus*', *Style and Idea: Selected Writings of Arnold Schoenberg*, ed. L. Stein (London, 1975), 481–2, 482–3

S. Karlinsky: 'Stravinsky and Russian Preliterate Theater', *19CM*, vi (1982–3), 232–40; also in *Confronting Stravinsky*, ed. J. Pasler (San Diego, 1982), 3–15

A. Lessem: 'Schoenberg, Stravinsky and Neo-Classicism: the Issues Reexamined', *MQ*, lxvii (1982), 527–42

R. Shattuck: 'The Devil's Dance: Stravinsky's Corporal Imagination', *Confronting Stravinsky*, ed. J. Pasler (San Diego, 1982), 82–8; repr. in R. Shattuck: *The Innocent Eye* (New York, 1984)

R. Taruskin: 'From Subject to Style: Stravinsky and the Painters', *Confronting Stravinsky*, ed. J. Pasler (San Diego, 1982), 16–38

L. Andriessen and E. Schönberger: *Het apollonisch uurwerk: over Stravinsky* (Amsterdam, 1983; Eng. trans., 1989, as *The Apollonian Clockwork: on Stravinsky*)

T.P. Gordon: *Stravinsky and the New Classicism: a Critical History, 1911–1928* (diss., U. of Toronto, 1983)

C. Geelhaar: 'Strawinsky und Picasso, zwei ebenbürtige Genies', *Strawinsky: sein Nachlass, sein Bild* (Basle, 1984), 285–304

R. Stephan: 'Zur Deutung von Strawinskys Neoclassizismus', *Igor Strawinsky*, Musik-Konzepte, nos.34–5 (1984), 80–88

S. Walsh: 'Review Survey: some Recent Stravinsky Literature', *MAn*, iii (1984), 201–8

W. Dömpling and T. Hirsbrunner: *Über Strawinsky: Studien zu Ästhetik und Kompositions-technik* (Laaber, 1985)

W. Austin: 'Stravinsky's "Fortunate Continuities" and "Legitimate Accidents", 1882–1982', *Stravinsky Retrospectives*, ed. E. Haimo and P. Johnson (Lincoln, NE, 1987), 1–14

C. Dahlhaus: 'Das Problem der "höherem Kritik": Adornos Polemik gegen Strawinsky', *NZM*, Jg.148, no.5 (1987), 9–15

C. Spies: 'Conundrums, Conjectures, Construals, or 5 vs. 3: the Influence of Russian Composers on Stravinsky', *Stravinsky Retrospectives*, ed. E. Haimo and P. Johnson (Lincoln, NE, 1987), 76–140

R. Taruskin: 'Stravinsky and the Traditions: Why the Memory Hole?', *Opus*, iii/4 (1987), 10–17

C. Deliège: 'Stravinsky: Ideology – Language', *PNM*, xxvi/1 (1988), 82–106

S. Messing: *Neoclassicism in Music* (Ann Arbor, 1988)

R. Taruskin: 'The Dark Side of Modern Music', *New Republic* (5 Sept 1988)

D. Albright: 'Stravinsky's Assault on Language', *JMR*, viii (1989), 259–79

D. Albright: *Stravinsky: The Music Box and the Nightingale* (New York, 1989)

V. Smirnov: 'Stravinsky: vsled za Musorgskim' [Stravinsky: in the steps of Musorgsky], *SovM* (1989), no.3, pp.86–91

R. Taruskin and R. Craft: 'Jews and Geniuses: an Exchange', *New York Review of Books* (15 June 1989)

A. Kurchenko: 'Stravinsky i Dostoyevsky', *SovM* (1990), no.3, pp.103–12

M. Kundera: 'Improvisation en hommage Stravinski', *L'infini*, no.36 (1991), 19–42; Eng. trans. in M. Kundera *Testaments Betrayed* (London and Boston, 1995), 55–98

P. Truman: 'An Aspect of Stravinsky's Russianism: Ritual', *RBM*, xlvi (1992), 225–46

G. Watkins: *Pyramids at the Louvre: Music, Culture and Collage from Stravinsky to the Postmodernists* (Cambridge, MA, 1994)

T.W. Adorno: 'Stravinsky: A Dialectical Portrait', *Quasi una fantasia: Essays on Modern Music*, trans. R. Livingstone (London, 1992), 145–75

R. Holloway: 'Customised Goods', *MT*, cxxxviii (1997), no.10, pp.21–5; no.11, pp.25–8; no.12, pp.21–5 [review of R. Taruskin: *Stravinsky and the Russian Traditions* (Berkeley and Oxford, 1996)]

R. Taruskin: 'Stravinsky and the Subhuman', *Defining Russia Musically* (Princeton, NJ, 1997), 360–467

J. Cross: *The Stravinsky Legacy* (Cambridge, 1998)

# I: Analytical studies

I. Glebov [B.V. Asaf'yev]: *Kniga O Stravinskom* [A book about Stravinsky] (Leningrad, 1929, 2/1977; Eng. trans., 1982)

O. Messiaen: 'Le rythme chez Igor Strawinsky', *ReM*, no.188–91 (1939), 331–2

P. Boulez: 'Stravinsky demeure', *Musique russe*, ed. P. Souvtchinsky (Paris, 1953), 151–224; repr. in P. Boulez: *Relevés d'apprenti* (Paris, 1966; Eng. trans., 1991), 75–145

R. Craft: 'Stravinsky's Revisions', *Counterpoint*, xviii (1953), 14–16

D. Drew: 'Stravinsky's Revisions', *The Score*, no.20 (1957), 47–58

R. Gerhard: 'Twelve-Note Technique in Stravinsky', ibid., 38–43

H. Keller: 'Rhythm: Gershwin and Stravinsky', ibid., 19–31

E.T. Cone: 'The Uses of Convention: Stravinsky and his Models', *MQ*, xlviii (1962), 287–99

R.U. Nelson: 'Stravinsky's Concept of Variations', ibid., 327–39

E.T. Cone: 'Stravinsky: the Progress of a Method', *PNM*, i/1 (1962–3), 18–26; repr. in *Perspectives on Schoenberg and Stravinsky*, ed. B. Boretz and E.T. Cone (Princeton, NJ, 1968, 2/1972), 156–64

M. Babbitt: 'Remarks on the Recent Stravinsky', *PNM*, ii/2 (1963–4), 35–55; repr. in *Perspectives on Schoenberg and Stravinsky*, ed. B. Boretz and E.T. Cone (Princeton, NJ, 1968, 2/1972), 165–85

A. Berger: 'Problems of Pitch Organization in Stravinsky', *PNM*, ii/1 (1963–4), 11–42; repr. in *Perspectives on Schoenberg and Stravinsky*, ed. B. Boretz and E.T. Cone (Princeton, NJ, 1968, 2/1972), 123–54

G.W. Hopkins: 'Stravinsky's Chords', *Tempo*, no.76 (1966), 6–12; no.77 (1966), 2–9

H. Pousseur: 'Stravinsky selon Webern selon Stravinsky', *Musique en jeu*, no.4 (1971), 21–47; no.5 (1971), 107–25; Eng. trans. in *PNM*, x/2 (1971–2), 13–51; xi/2 (1972–3), 112–45

V. Cholopova [Kholopova]: 'Russische Quellen der Rhythmik Strawinskys', *Mf*, xxvii (1974), 435–46

P.C. van den Toorn: 'Some Characteristics of Stravinsky's Diatonic Music', *PNM*, xiv/1 (1975–6), 104–38; xv/2 (1976–7), 58–95

M. Babbitt: 'Order, Symmetry, and Centricity in Late Stravinsky', *Confronting Stravinsky*, ed. J. Pasler (San Diego, 1982), 247–61

A. Forte: 'Harmonic Syntax and Voice Leading in Stravinsky's Early Music', ibid., 95–129

J.D. Kramer: 'Discontinuity and Proportion in the Music of Stravinsky', ibid., 174–94

J. Straus: 'A Principle of Voice Leading in the Music of Stravinsky', *Music Theory Spectrum*, iv (1982), 106–24

J. Straus: 'Stravinsky's Tonal Axis', *JMT*, xxvi (1982), 261–90

P.C. van den Toorn: 'Octatonic Pitch Structure in Stravinsky', *Confronting Stravinsky*, ed. J. Pasler (San Diego, 1982), 130–56

G. Watkins: 'The Canon and Stravinsky's Late Style', ibid., 217–46

C. Wuorinen and J. Kresky: 'On the Significance of Stravinsky's Last Works', ibid., 262–70

M. Zur: 'Tonal Ambiguities as a Constructive Force in the Music of Stravinsky', *MQ*, lxviii (1982), 516–26

M. Kielian-Gilbert: 'Relationships of Symmetrical Pitch-Class Sets and Stravinsky's Metaphor of Polarity', *PNM*, xxi (1982–3), 210–21

P.C. van den Toorn: *The Music of Igor Stravinsky* (New Haven, CT, 1983)

R. Taruskin: 'Chernomor to Kashchei: Harmonic Sorcery, or Stravinsky's "Angle"', *JAMS*, xxxviii (1985), 72–142

E. Antokoletz: 'Interval Cycles in Stravinsky's Early Ballets', *JAMS*, xxxix (1986), 578–614

J.N. Cholopow [Kholopov]: 'Die Harmonik im Frühwerk Strawinskys', *BMw*, xxviii (1986), 251–66

M. Karallus: *Igor Strawinsky: der übergang zur seriellen Kompositionstechnik* (Tutzing, 1986)

R. Taruskin: '*Chez Petrouchka*: Harmony and Tonality *chez* Stravinsky', *19CM*, x (1986–7), 265–86

M. Babbitt: 'Stravinsky's Verticals and Schoenberg's Diagonals: a Twist of Fate', *Stravinsky Retrospectives*, ed. E. Haimo and P. Johnson (Lincoln, NE, 1987), 15–35

P. Johnson: 'Cross-Collectional Techniques of Structure in Stravinsky's Centric Music', ibid., 55–75

M. Kielian-Gilbert: 'The Rhythms of Form: Correspondence and Analogy in Stravinsky's Designs', *Music Theory Spectrum*, ix (1987), 42–66

J.N. Straus: 'Sonata Form in Stravinsky', *Stravinsky Retrospectives*, ed. E. Haimo and P. Johnson (Lincoln, NE, 1987), 141–61

R. Taruskin: 'Stravinsky's "Rejoicing Discovery" and What it Meant: in Defense of his Notorious Text Setting', ibid., 162–99

P.C. van den Toorn: *Stravinsky and 'The Rite of Spring': the Beginnings of a Musical Language* (Berkeley, 1987)

P.C. van den Toorn: 'Taruskin's Angle', *In Theory Only*, x/3 (1987), 27–46

J.D. Kramer: *The Time of Music* (New York, 1988)

P.C. van den Toorn: 'Stravinsky Rebarred', *MAn*, vii (1988), 165–95

V.K. Agawu: 'Stravinsky's *Mass* and Stravinsky Analysis', *Music Theory Spectrum*, xi (1989), 139–63

P.C. van den Toorn: 'Context and Analytical Method in Stravinsky', *Music, Politics and the Academy* (Berkeley and Los Angeles, 1995), 179–219

L. Rogers: 'Stravinsky's break with contrapuntal tradition: a sketch study', *JM* xiii (1995), 476–507

A. Pople: *Skryabin and Stravinsky, 1908–1914: Studies in Theory and Analysis* (New York and London, 1989)

A. Whittall: 'Review Survey: some Recent Writings on Stravinsky', *MAn*, viii (1989), 169–76

R. Graybill: 'Intervallic Transformation and Closure in the Music of Stravinsky', *Theory and Practice*, xiv–xv (1989–90), 13–34

J.N. Straus: *Remaking the Past: Musical Modernism and the Influence of the Tonal Tradition* (Cambridge, MA, 1990)

M. Kielian-Gilbert: 'Stravinsky's Contrasts: Contradiction and Discontinuity in his Neoclassic Music', *JM*, ix (1991), 448–80

G.G. Horlacher: 'The Rhythms of Reiteration: Formal Development in Stravinsky's Ostinati', *Music Theory Spectrum*, xiv (1992), 171–87

L. Rogers: 'Varied Repetition and Stravinsky's Compositional Process', *Mitteilungen der Paul Sacher Stiftung*, vii (1994), 22–6

P.C. van den Toorn: 'Context and Analytical Method in Stravinsky', *Music, Politics and the Academy* (Berkeley and Los Angeles, 1995), 179–219

L. Rogers: 'Stravinsky's break with contrapuntal tradition: a sketch study', *JM*, xiii (1995), 476–507

A. Pople: 'Misleading Voices: Contrasts and Continuities in Stravinsky Studies', *Analytical Strategies and Musical Interpretation*, ed. C. Ayrey and M. Everist (Cambridge, 1996), 271–87

G. Schröder: *Cadenza und Concerto: Studien zu Igor Strawinskijs Instrumentalismus um 1920* (Cologne, 1996)

J.N. Straus: 'Babbitt and Stravinsky under the Serial "Regime"', *PNM*, xxxv/2 (1997), 17–32

# J: Ballets

## General

A.N. Rimsky-Korsakov: 'Baletï Igorya Stravinskogo', *Apollon* (1915), no.1, pp.46–57

A. Levinson: 'Stravinsky et la danse', *ReM*, v/1–2 (1923–4), 155–65

M. Lederman, ed.: *Stravinsky in the Theatre* (New York, 1949)

I.Ya. Vershinina: *Ranniye baletï Stravinskogo* [The early ballets of Stravinsky] (Moscow, 1967)

H. Kirchmeyer: *Stravinskys russische Ballette* (Stuttgart, 1974)

D. Hockney: 'Set Designing for Stravinsky', *Confronting Stravinsky*, ed. J. Pasler (San Diego, 1982), 89–91

J. Pasler: 'Music and Spectacle in *Petrushka* and *The Rite of Spring*', ibid., 53–81

E. Antokoletz: 'Interval Cycles in Stravinsky's Early Ballets', *JAMS*, xxxix (1986), 578–614

## The Rite of Spring

J. Rivière: 'Le sacre du printemps', *Nouvelle revue française*, iv (1913), 700–30; repr. in J. Rivière: *Nouvelles études* (Paris, 1947)

J. Cocteau: *Le coq et l'arlequin* (Paris, 1918)

P. Boulez: 'Stravinsky demeure', *Musique russe*, ed. P. Souvtchinsky (Paris, 1953); repr. in P. Boulez: *Relevés d'apprenti* (Paris, 1966; Eng. trans., 1991), 75–145

J. Barraqué: 'Rythme et développement', *Polyphonie*, nos.9–10 (1954), 47–73

I. Stravinsky and R. Craft: *Le sacre du printemps: Sketches 1911–1913* (London, 1969) [incl. commentary and essays by Craft]

R. Smalley: 'The Sketchbook of The Rite of Spring', *Tempo*, no.91 (1969–70), 2–13

A. Schaeffner: 'Au fil des esquisses du "Sacre"', *RdM*, lvii (1971), 179–90

A. Forte: *The Harmonic Organization of 'The Rite of Spring'* (New Haven, CT, 1978); see also reviews by R. Craft, *MQ*, lxiv (1978), 524–35, and R. Taruskin, *CMc*, no.28 (1979), 114–29

L. Morton: 'Footnotes to Stravinsky Studies: *Le sacre du printemps*', *Tempo* no.128 (1979), 9–16

F. Lesure, ed.: *Igor Stravinsky: Le sacre du printemps: dossier de presse* (Geneva, 1980)

R. Taruskin: 'Russian Folk Melodies in *The Rite of Spring*', *JAMS*, xxxiii (1980), 501–43

L. Cyr: '*Le sacre du printemps*: petite histoire d'une grande partition', *Stravinsky: études & témoignages*, ed. F. Lesure (Paris, 1982), 89–147

L. Cyr: 'Writing *The Rite* Right', *Confronting Stravinsky*, ed. J. Pasler (San Diego, 1982), 157–73

V. Scherliess: *Igor Stravinsky: Le sacre du printemps* (Munich, 1982)

A. Whittall: 'Music Analysis as Human Science? *Le sacre du printemps* in theory and practice', *MAn*, i (1982), 33–53

R. Taruskin: 'The Rite revisited: the idea and sources of its scenario', *Music and Civilization: Essays in Honor of Paul Henry Lang,* ed. E. Strainchamps and M.R. Maniates (New York, 1984), 183–202

P.C. van den Toorn: *Stravinsky and 'The Rite of Spring': the Beginnings of a Musical Language* (Berkeley, 1987)

S.C. Berg: *Le Sacre du printemps: seven productions from Nijinsky to Martha Graham* (Ann Arbor, 1988)

J. Acocella, L. Garafola, J. Greene: 'The Rite of Spring considered as a nineteenth-century ballet', *Ballet Review*, xx/2 (Summer, 1992)

F.C. Ricci: 'Canudo e Stravinskij', *Ottocento e oltre: scritti in onore di Raoul Meloncelli*, ed. F. Izzo and J. Streicher (Rome, 1993), 535–42

## The Wedding

V. Belaiev: *Igor Stravinsky's 'Les noces'* (London, 1928)

N. Goncharova: 'The Creation of "Les noces"', *Ballet and Opera* (1949), Sept, 23–6

H. Lindlar: 'Christ-kultische Elemente in Strawinskys Bauernhochzeit', *Melos*, xxv (1958), 63–6

B. Nijinska: 'Creation of "Les noces"', *Dance Magazine* (1974), Dec, 58–61

N. Nabokov: 'The Peasant Marriage (*Les noces*) by Igor Stravinsky', *Slavic Studies of the Hebrew University of Jerusalem*, iii (1978), 272–81

N. Goncharova: 'The Metamorphoses of the Ballet "Les noces"', *Leonardo*, xii (1979), 137–43

M. Mazo: 'Stravinsky's *Les noces* and Russian Village Wedding Ritual', *JAMS*, xliii (1990), 99–142

J. Jaubert: 'Some Ideas about Meter in the Fourth Tableau of Stravinsky's *Les Noces*, or Stravinsky, Nijinska, and Particle Physics', *MQ*, lxxxiii (1999), 205–26

### Other works

E. Evans: *Stravinsky: 'The Fire-Bird' and 'Petrushka'* (London, 1933)

F.W. Sternfeld: 'Some Russian Folk Songs in Stravinsky's Petrouchka', *Notes* (1945)

A. Dennington: 'The Three Orchestrations of Stravinsky's "Firebird"', *The Chesterian*, xxxiv (1960), 89–94

L. Morton: 'Stravinsky and Tchaikovsky: "Le baiser de la fée"', *MQ*, xlviii (1962), 313–26; repr. in *Stravinsky: a New Appraisal of his Work*, ed. P.H. Lang (New York, 1962), 47–60

H. Pousseur: 'Stravinsky selon Webern selon Stravinsky', *Musique en jeu*, no.4 (1971), 21–47; no.5 (1971), 107–25; Eng. trans. in *PNM*, x/2 (1971–2), 13–51; xi/2 (1972–3), 112–45 [on *Agon*]

R. Taruskin: '*Chez Petrouchka*: Harmony and Tonality *chez* Stravinsky', *19CM*, x (1986–7), 265–86

A.I. Klimovitsky: 'Ob odnom neizvestnom avtografe I. Stravinskogo (k probleme tvorcheskogo formirovaniya kompozitora)' [An unknown Stravinsky autograph (concerning the problem of the composer's creative development)], *Pamyatniki kul 'turï: novïye otkrïtiya 1986* (Leningrad, 1987), 227–36 [on *Firebird*]

B.S. Brook: 'Stravinsky's *Pulcinella*: the "Pergolesi" Sources', *Musiques, signes, images: liber amicorum François Lesure*, ed. J.-M. Fauquet (Geneva, 1988), 41–66

I. Alm: 'Stravinsky, Balanchine and *Agon*: an Analysis based on the Collaborative Process', *JM*, vii (1989), 254–69

V.V. Smirnov: '… c'est du Tchaïkowsky à travers Stravinsky', *Mitteilungen der Paul Sacher Stiftung*, vii (1994), 27–9 [on *Le baiser de la fée*]

S. Savenko: '*L'oiseau de feu*: zur Geschichte der ersten Fassung', *Mitteilungen der Paul Sacher Stiftung*, viii (1995), 31–5

D. Bruce: 'Source and Sorcery', *MT*, cxxxvii (1996), 11–15 [on *Le baiser de la fée*]

# K: Operas

### Mavra

F. Poulenc: 'La Musique: à propos de "Mavra" de Igor Stravinsky', *Feuilles libres*, no.27 (1922), 223–5

A. Lourié: 'Dve operï Stravinskogo', *Vyorstï*, iii (1928), 109–21

S. Campbell: 'The "Mavras" of Pushkin, Kochno and Stravinsky', *ML*, lviii (1977), 304–21

**The Rake's Progress**

P. Griffiths: *Igor Stravinsky: The Rake's Progress* (Cambridge, 1982)

D. Albright: *Stravinsky: The Music Box and the Nightingale* (New York, 1989), 42–81

M. Hunter: 'Igor and Tom: History and Destiny in *The Rake's Progress*', *OQ*, vii/4 (1990–91), 38–52

J.N. Straus: 'The Progress of a Motive in Stravinsky's *The Rake's Progress*', *JM*, ix (1991), 165–85

N. John (ed.): *Oedipus Rex, The Rake's Progress: Igor Stravinsky*, ENO Opera Guide (London, 1991)

V. Scherliess: 'Mozart à la Strawinsky: zu einer Melodie aus *The Rake's Progress*', *Mitteilungen der Paul Sacher Stiftung*, v (1992), 14–18

G. Chew: 'Pastoral and Neoclassicism: a Reinterpretation of Auden's and Stravinsky's *Rake's Progress*', *COJ*, v (1993), 239–63

V. Scherliess: '"Inspiration" und "Fabrication": Beobachtungen zu Igor Strawinskys Arbeit an *The Rake's Progress*', *Quellenstudien II: zwölf Komponisten des 20. Jahrhunderts*, ed. F. Meyer (Winterthur, 1993), 39–72

S. Walsh: 'Venice and *The Rake*: the old and the new', *The Rake's Progress* (Welsh National Opera programme book) (Cardiff, 1996), 21–6

C. Carter: 'Stravinsky's "Special Sense": the Rhetorical Use of Tonality in *The Rake's Progress*', *Music Theory Spectrum*, xix (1997), 55–80

# L: Other dramatic works

### Histoire Du Soldat

E. Ansermet: 'L'histoire du soldat', *The Chesterian*, x (1920), 289–95

L. Pitoëff: 'Souvenirs intimes de "L'histoire du soldat"', *Quartier Latin* [Montreal] (23 March 1945)

J. Jacquot: '"Histoire du Soldat": la genèse du texte et la représentation de 1918', *Voies de la création théâtrale*, vi (1978), 79–142

C.F. Ramuz and R. Auberjonois: 'Autour de l'*Histoire du soldat*', *Etudes de lettres* (1978), no.4, pp.87–93

R. Craft: '*Histoire du soldat*: the Musical Revisions, the Sketches, the Evolution of the Libretto', *MQ*, lxvi (1980), 321–38

B. Heyman: 'Stravinsky and Ragtime', *MQ*, lxviii (1982), 543–62

H. Wagner: 'Igor Strawinsky und René Auberjonois', *Strawinsky: sein Nachlass, sein Bild* (Basle, 1984), 307–74

J. Evans: '"Diabolus triumphans": Stravinsky's *Histoire du soldat* in Weimar and Nazi Germany', *Varieties of Musicology: Essays for Murray Lefkowitz*, ed. J. Daverio and J. Ogasapian (Warren, MI, 1999), 179–89

### Other works

A. Lourié: '*Oedipus-Rex* de Strawinsky', *ReM*, viii/8 (1927), 240–53

A. Lourié: 'Dve operï Stravinskogo', *Vyorstï*, iii (1928), 109–21 [on *Oedipus Rex*]

J. Claude: 'Autour de Perséphone', *Bulletin des Amis d'André Gide*, xv (1987), 23–55

A.D. McCredie: 'Form als Symbolik in Igor Strawinskys *Die Flut*', *Musikkulturgeschichte: Festschrift für Constantin Floros*, ed. P. Petersen (Wiesbaden, 1990), 213–32

P. Pollard: '*Sit Tityrus Orpheus*: Gide et la musique', *Bulletin des Amis d'André Gide*, xviii (1990), 17–64 [on *Perséphone*]

N. John (ed.): *Oedipus Rex, The Rake's Progress: Igor Stravinsky*. ENO Opera Guide (London, 1991)

S. Walsh: *Stravinsky: Oedipus Rex* (Cambridge, 1993)

## M: Orchestral and large ensemble works

### Symphonies d'instruments à vent

E.T. Cone: 'Stravinsky: the Progress of a Method', *PNM*, i/1 (1962–3), 18–26; repr. in *Perspectives on Schoenberg and Stravinsky*, ed. B. Boretz and E.T. Cone (Princeton, NJ, 1968, 2/1972), 156–64

L. Somfai: '*Symphonies of Wind Instruments* (1920): Observations on Stravinsky's Organic Construction', *SM*, xiv (1972), 355–83

J.D. Kramer: 'Linearity, Nonlinearity and Moment Time in Stravinsky's *Symphonies of Wind Instruments*', *The Time of Music* (New York, 1988), 221–85

V. Scherliess: 'Zur Arbeitsweise Igor Strawinskys dargestellt an den "Symphonies d'instruments à vent"', *Vom Einfall zum Kunstwerk*, ed. H. Danuser and G. Katzenberger (Laaber, 1993), 161–85

S. Walsh: 'Stravinsky's Symphonies: Accident or Design?', *Analytical Strategies and Musical Interpretation*, ed. C. Ayrey and M. Everist (Cambridge, 1996), 35–71

A. Rehding: 'Towards a Logic of Discontinuity in Stravinsky's *Symphonies of Wind Instruments*', *MAn*, xvii (1998), 39–65

### Other works

J. Druckman: 'Stravinsky's Orchestral Style', *Juilliard Review*, iv/2 (1957), 10–19

A. Briner: 'Guillaume de Machaut 1958/9, oder Strawinskys "Movements for Piano and Orchestra"', *Melos*, xi (1960), 184–6

H. Keller: 'No Bridge to Nowhere', *MT*, cii (1961), 156–8 [on *Movements*]

E.T. Cone: 'The Uses of Convention: Stravinsky and his Models', *MQ*, xlviii (1962), 287–99 [on Symphony in C]

C. Spies: 'Notes on Stravinsky's Variations', *PNM*, iv/1 (1965–6), 62–74; repr. in *Perspectives on Schoenberg and Stravinsky*, ed. B. Boretz and E.T. Cone (Princeton, NJ, 1968, 2/1972), 210–22

B.M. Williams: 'Time and the Structure of Stravinsky's Symphony in C', *MQ*, lix (1973), 355–69

W.E. Benjamin: 'Tonality without 5ths: Remarks on the First Movement of Stravinsky's Concerto for Piano and Wind Instruments', *In Theory Only*, ii (1977), 53–70

R.P. Morgan: 'Dissonant Prolongations, Perfect 5ths and Major 3rds in Stravinsky's Piano Concerto', *In Theory Only*, iv (1978), 3–7

B. Schwarz: 'Stravinsky, Dushkin, and the Violin', *Confronting Stravinsky*, ed. J. Pasler (San Diego, 1982), 302–9

P.S. Phillips: 'The Enigma of *Variations*: a study of Stravinsky's Final Work for Orchestra', *MAn*, iii (1984), 69–89

P. Hollerbach: 'The Genesis of Stravinsky's *Ebony Concerto*', *Peabody Essays in Music History*, ii (1989), 37–79

K.D. Wile: 'Communication and Interaction in Stravinsky's *Scherzo fantastique*', *Indiana Theory Review*, xiii (1992), 87–112

P. Dunnigan: 'Stravinsky and the *Circus Polka*', *Journal of Band Research*, xxx (1994), 35–52

V. Rilke: 'Strawinskys Auseinandersetzung mit der Sonatensatzform: der Kopfsatz der *Symphony in Three Movements*', *Mf*, xlvii (1994), 42–57

D. Rust: 'Stravinsky's Twelve-Tone Loom: Composition and Precomposition in *Movements*', *Music Theory Spectrum*, xvi/1 (1994), 62–76

L. Rogers: 'Stravinsky's Break with Contrapuntal Tradition: a Sketch Study', *JM*, xiii/4 (1995), 476–506 [on Violin Concerto]

# N: Vocal and choral works

R. Craft: 'Stravinsky's Mass: a Notebook', *Igor Stravinsky*, ed. E. Corle (New York, 1949), 201–6

R. Vlad: 'Le musiche sacre di Strawinsky', *RaM*, xxii (1952), 212–19

R. Craft: 'A Concert for Saint Mark', *The Score*, no.18 (1956), 35–51 [on *Canticum sacrum*]

R. Craft, A. Piovesan and R. Vlad: *Le musiche religiose di Igor Stravinsky* (Venice, 1956)

H. Boys: 'A Note on Stravinsky's Settings of English', *The Score*, no.20 (1957), 14–19

H. Lindlar: *Igor Strawinskys sakraler Gesang: Geist und Form der christkultischen Kompositionen* (Regensburg, 1957)

C. Spies: 'Some Notes on Stravinsky's Requiem Settings', *PNM*, v/2 (1966–7), 98–123; repr. in *Perspectives on Schoenberg and Stravinsky*, ed. B. Boretz and E.T. Cone (Princeton, NJ, 1968, 2/1972), 223–49

H. Lindlar: 'Die frühen Lieder von Strawinsky', *Musica*, xxiii (1969), 116–18

T. Clifton: 'Types of Symmetrical Relations in Stravinsky's *A Sermon, a Narrative, and a Prayer*', *PNM*, ix/1 (1970–71), 96–112

R. Holloway: 'Stravinsky's Self-Concealment', *Tempo*, no.108 (1974), 2–10

L. Somfai: 'Sprache, Wort und Phonem im vokalen Spätwerk Strawinskys', *Veroffentlichung des Instituts für neue Musik und Musikerziehung Darmstadt*, xiv (1974), 34–44

G. Amy: 'Aspects of the Religious Music of Igor Stravinsky', *Confronting Stravinsky*, ed. J. Pasler (San Diego, 1982), 195–206

T. Funayama: '*Three Japanese Lyrics* and Japonisme', ibid., 273–83

C. Hogan: '"Threni": Stravinsky's "Debt" to Krenek', *Tempo*, no.141 (1982), 22–9

V.K. Agawu: 'Stravinsky's *Mass* and Stravinsky Analysis', *Music Theory Spectrum*, xi (1989), 139–63

J.N. Straus: 'Two "Mistakes" in Stravinsky's *Introitus*', *Mitteilungen der Paul Sacher Stiftung*, iv (1991), 34–6

G. Schliess: *Igor Strawinskys frühe Lieder* (Regensburg, 1992)

I. Vershinina: 'Bal'mont i Stravinsky', *MAk* (1992), no.4, pp.182–4

I. Vershinina: '"Zvezdolikiy": odin iz avtographov' [One of the autographs], *MAk* (1992), no.4, pp.135–9

R. Taruskin: 'The Traditional Revisited: Stravinsky's *Requiem Canticles* as Russian Music', *Music Theory and the Exploration of the Past*, ed. C. Hatch and D.W. Bernstein (Chicago, 1993), 525–50

D.H. Smyth: 'Stravinsky at the Threshold: a Sketch Leaf for *Canticum sacrum*', *Mitteilungen der Paul Sacher Stiftung*, x (1997), 21–6

## O: Chamber and solo instrumental works

A. Lourié: 'La Sonate pour piano de Strawinsky', *ReM*, vi/9–11 (1924–5), 100–14

A. Cortot: 'Igor Strawinsky, le piano et les pianistes', *ReM*, no.188–91 (1939), 264–308

E. Stein: 'Stravinsky's Septet (1953): an Analysis', *Tempo*, no.31 (1954), 7–11

D.C. Johns: 'An Early Serial Idea of Stravinsky', *MR*, xxiii (1962), 305–13 [on Sonata for Two Pianos]

C. Burkhart: 'Stravinsky's Revolving Canon', *MR*, xxix (1968), 161–6 [on Sonata for Two Pianos]

C.M. Joseph: 'Stravinsky's Piano Scherzo (1902) in Perspective: a New Starting Point', *MQ*, lxvii (1981), 82–93

B. Heyman: 'Stravinsky and Ragtime', *MQ*, lxviii (1982), 543–62

F.W. Hoogerwerf: 'Tonal and Referential Aspects of Set in Stravinsky's Septet', *JMR*, iv (1982), 69–84

C.M. Joseph: 'Structural Coherence in Stravinsky's *Piano-Rag-Music*', *Music Theory Spectrum*, iv (1982), 76–91

C. Joseph: *Stravinsky and the Piano* (Ann Arbor, 1983)

E. Haimo: 'Problems of Hierarchy in Stravinsky's *Octet*', *Stravinsky Retrospectives*, ed. E. Haimo and P. Johnson (Lincoln, NE, 1987), 36–54

W. Hays: 'On Voice-Leading and Syntax in the "Cadenza Finale" from Stravinsky's *Sérénade en la*', *Theory and Practice*, xii (1987), 55–65

R. Hermann: 'Thoughts on Voice-Leading and Set Theory in "Neo-Tonal" Works: the "Hymne" from Stravinsky's *Sérénade en la*', ibid., 27–53

M. Kielian-Gilbert: 'Patterns of Repetition in the Hymne of Stravinsky's *Sérénade en la*', ibid., 11–25

J.N. Straus: 'The Problem of Coherence in Stravinsky's *Sérénade en la*', ibid., 3–10

B.J. Boettcher: *A Study of Stravinsky's Sonate pour piano and Sérénade en la* (San Francisco, 1991)

D. Puffett: 'Too Sharp a Mind', *MT*, cxxxvi (1995), 591–8 [on Septet]

R. Sievers: *Igor Strawinsky: Trois pièces pour quatuor à cordes: Analyse und Deutung* (Wiesbaden, 1996)

## P: Arrangements

M. Ravel: 'O parizhskoy redaktsii "Khovanshchina"' [On the Paris edition of *Khovanshchina*], *Muzika*, no.129 (1913), 338–42

R. Craft: 'A Note on Gesualdo's "Sacrae Cantiones" and on Gesualdo and Strawinsky', *Tempo*, no.45 (1957), 5–7

R. Threlfall: 'The Stravinsky Version of *Khovanshchina*', *Studies in Music*, xv (1981), 106–15

A.I. Klimovitsky: 'Dve "Pesni o blokhe" – Bětkhovena i Musorgskogo – v instrumentovke Stravinskogo' [Two songs about a flea – Beethoven and Musorgsky – in Stravinsky's orchestration], *Pamyatniki kul'turï: novïye otkrïtiya 1984* (Leningrad, 1986), 196–216

## Q: Iconography

M. Cosman and H. Keller: *Stravinsky at Rehearsal* (London, 1962, enlarged 1982, as *Stravinsky Seen and Heard* )

A. Newman and R. Craft: *Bravo Stravinsky* (New York, 1967)

T. Strawinsky: *Catherine & Igor Stravinsky: a Family Album* (London, 1973)

V. Stravinsky, R. McCaffrey and R. Craft: *Igor and Vera Stravinsky: a Photograph Album 1921 to 1971* (London, 1982)

R. Craft: *A Stravinsky Scrapbook 1940–1971* (London, 1983)

J.E. Bowlt, ed.: *The Salon Album of Vera Sudeikin-Stravinsky* (Princeton, NJ, 1995)

## R: Reception history

T. Bullard: *The First Performance of Igor Stravinsky's 'Rite of Spring'* (diss., U. of Rochester, 1971)

D. Bancroft: 'Stravinsky and the "NRF" (1920–29)', *ML*, liii (1972), 274–83; lv (1974), 261–71

J. Pasler: 'Stravinsky and his Craft: Trends in Stravinsky Criticism and Research', *MT*, cxxiv (1983), 605–9

A. Kuznetsov: 'Muzïka Stravinskogo na konsertnoy estrade Rossii' [Stravinsky's music on the Russian concert platform], *MAk* (1992), no.4, pp.119–27

S. Walsh: 'Stravinsky and the Vicious Circle', *Composition – Performance – Reception*, ed. W. Thomas (Aldershot and Brookfield, VE, 1998), 132–44

J. Evans: 'Some Remarks on the Publication and Reception of Stravinsky's *Erinnerungen*', *Mitteilungen der Paul Sacher Stiftung*, ix (1996), 17–23

J. Evans: 'Die Rezeption der Musik Igor Strawinskys in Hitlerdeutschland', *AMw*, lv (1998), 91–109

# INDEX